MODEL DOUBLE TAXATION CONVENTION
ON ESTATES AND INHERITANCES
AND ON GIFTS

ORGANISATION FOR ECONOMIC CO-OPERATION AND DEVELOPMENT

Pursuant to article 1 of the Convention signed in Paris on 14th December, 1960, and which came into force on 30th September, 1961, the Organisation for Economic Co-operation and Development (OECD) shall promote policies designed:

- to achieve the highest sustainable economic growth and employment and a rising standard of living in Member countries, while maintaining financial stability, and thus to contribute to the development of the world economy;
- to contribute to sound economic expansion in Member as well as non-member countries in the process of economic development; and
- to contribute to the expansion of world trade on a multilateral, non-discriminatory basis in accordance with international obligations.

The Signatories of the Convention on the OECD are Austria, Belgium, Canada, Denmark, France, the Federal Republic of Germany, Greece, Iceland, Ireland, Italy, Luxembourg, the Netherlands, Norway, Portugal, Spain, Sweden, Switzerland, Turkey, the United Kingdom and the United States. The following countries acceded subsequently to this Convention (the dates are those on which the instruments of accession were deposited): Japan (28th April, 1964), Finland (28th January, 1969), Australia (7th June, 1971) and New Zealand (29th May, 1973).

The Socialist Federal Republic of Yugoslavia takes part in certain work of the OECD (agreement of 28th October, 1961).

Publié en français sous le titre:

MODÈLE DE CONVENTION
DE DOUBLE IMPOSITION
CONCERNANT
LES SUCCESSIONS ET LES DONATIONS

This report has been prepared by the Committee on Fiscal Affairs between 1978 and 1982 as part of its programme of work on double taxation, with a view to up-dating and extending to gift taxation the 1966 OECD Draft Double Taxation Convention on Estates and Inheritances.

The Council of the OECD adopted on 3rd June, 1982 a Recommendation concerning the avoidance of double taxation with respect to taxes on Estates and Inheritances and on Gifts (see Appendix I) and agreed to the publication of the report.

Also available

REVENUE STATISTICS OF OECD MEMBER COUNTRIES 1965-1981 (August 1982)
(23 82 01 3) ISBN 92-64-02328-3 Bilingual   210 pages   £8.60   US$17.50   F86.00

INCOME TAX SCHEDULES – DISTRIBUTION OF TAXPAYERS AND REVENUES (December 1981)
(23 81 03 1) ISBN 92-64-12257-5   42 pages   £2.90   US$6.50   F29.00

TRANSFER PRICING AND MULTINATIONAL ENTERPRISES (July 1979)
(21 79 01 1) ISBN 92-64-11947-7   100 pages   £4.40   US$9.00   F36.00

THE TAXATION OF NET WEALTH, CAPITAL TRANSFERS AND CAPITAL GAINS OF INDIVIDUALS (March 1979)
(23 79 01 1) ISBN 92-64-11896-9   196 pages   £10.80   US$22.00   F88.00

MODEL DOUBLE TAXATION CONVENTION ON INCOME AND CAPITAL (September 1977)
(23 77 01 1) ISBN 92-64-11693-1   216 pages   £6.00   US$12.50   F50.00

Prices charged at the OECD Publications Office.

THE OECD CATALOGUE OF PUBLICATIONS and supplements will be sent free of charge on request addressed either to OECD Publications Office,
2, rue André-Pascal, 75775 PARIS CEDEX 16, or to the OECD Sales Agent in your country.

DETAILED LIST OF CONTENTS

COMMENTARY OF THE MODEL CONVENTION

APPENDICES

Part I

INTRODUCTORY REPORT
BY THE COMMITTEE ON FISCAL AFFAIRS

I

INTRODUCTION

1.   The Council of the Organisation for Economic Co-operation and Development adopted, on 30th July, 1963, a Recommendation concerning a Draft Convention for the avoidance of Double Taxation on Income and Capital (hereinafter called the 1963 Income Tax Draft). Following the same approach, the Council adopted, on 28th June, 1966, a Recommendation concerning a Draft Convention for the avoidance of Double Taxation on Estates and Inheritances (hereinafter called the 1966 Estate Tax Draft).

2.   Due to the fact that certain questions had not been entirely solved, the Fiscal Committee had planned to revise the 1963 Income Tax Draft in the light of the experience that had been gained. This work was started by the Fiscal Committee and was continued by its successor, the Committee on Fiscal Affairs, whose report led the Council of the Organisation to adopt, on 11th April, 1977, a new Recommendation concerning the avoidance of double taxation with respect to taxes on income and on capital and presenting a new Model Convention (hereinafter called the 1977 Income Tax Model)[1].

3.   The Committee on Fiscal Affairs then started a revision of the 1966 Estate Tax Draft, with a view to take account of recent trends in Member countries' attitudes towards the avoidance of double taxation with respect to taxes on estates and inheritances and on gifts and to adapt the 1966 Draft, where necessary, to the substance and form of the 1977 Income Tax Model. This work resulted in the present report, which contains a new Model Double Taxation Convention on Estates and Inheritances and on Gifts (hereinafter called the 1982 Estate Tax Model), accompanied by a recast of the Commentaries. The main feature of the new Model, when compared with the former Draft, is that taxes on gifts *inter vivos* are now included within the scope of the Convention.

4.   The conclusions of the report contain concrete recommendations of the Committee on Fiscal Affairs in order that the implementation of the new Model Convention may result in further progress towards harmonization of bilateral conventions and elimination of double taxation. The Council of the OECD has endorsed these views and adopted, on 3rd June, 1982, a Recommendation to that effect (see Appendix I).

---

1.   Model Double Taxation Convention on Income and on Capital, OECD, Paris 1977.

II

IMPLEMENTATION OF THE 1966 ESTATE TAX DRAFT

5.   The harmful effects of double taxation on the exchange of goods and services and movements of capital are well known and it is superfluous to stress the need to remove the obstacles that double taxation presents to the development of economic relations between the Member countries of the OECD. In this respect it is obvious that the effort to eliminate double taxation between Member countries needs to go beyond the field of periodic taxes on income and capital.

6.   Although taxes on estates and inheritances and on gifts are imposed only on specific events, the burden of taxation resulting from the simultaneous levy of the taxes imposed under the domestic laws of several countries is certainly prejudicial to the development of economic relations and in particular to movements of private capital between Member countries. It is therefore important also in the case of taxes on estates and inheritances and on gifts that persons in each Member country who engage in commercial, industrial or financial activities in the other Member countries, or more generally, who own property in such countries, should have their fiscal situation clarified, standardized and made secure through the application by all Member countries of common solutions for eliminating double taxation[2].

7.   Although the network of double taxation conventions applying to taxes on estates and inheritances is smaller than that covering taxes on income, the 1966 Estate Tax Draft has also had significant repercussions since Member countries have largely conformed to it when concluding or revising bilateral conventions (see Table).

8.   The importance of the work of the Fiscal Committee and now of the Committee on Fiscal Affairs should not be measured merely by the number of conventions concluded between Member countries but also by the fact that, in accordance with the Recommendations of the Council of the OECD, these conventions follow the pattern and, in most cases, the main provisions of the Model Conventions. These Model Conventions have facilitated bilateral negotiations between Member countries and achieved a desirable harmonization in bilateral conventions for the benefit of both taxpayers and national administrations. Moreover, the Commentaries have facilitated the interpretation and application of bilateral conventions along common lines.

9.   In presenting in 1977 a new Income Tax Model, the Committee on Fiscal Affairs sought to take advantage of the experience gained in the field of double taxation of income and capital to clarify some of the provisions contained in the 1963 Income Tax Draft and also to adapt it to the new developments within the domestic laws of Member countries.

---

2.   As to the historical background to the efforts to remove double taxation in general, reference is made to paragraphs 3-6 of the Introduction to the 1977 Income Tax Model.

10.   The Committee on Fiscal Affairs then decided to revise the 1966 Estate Tax Draft with the aim of bringing it into line with the 1977 Income Tax Model and to improve it wherever the need arose.

11.   The reasons for avoiding double taxation in respect of death duties also hold true for taxes on gifts *inter vivos* since such taxes are in some respects very similar to, and are moreover closely interconnected with, death duties in many countries. The Committee on Fiscal Affairs decided therefore that the time had come to include taxes on gifts *inter vivos* within the framework of a Model Convention.

NETWORK OF BILATERAL CONVENTIONS FOR AVOIDANCE OF DOUBLE TAXATION WITH RESPECT TO TAXES ON ESTATES AND INHERITANCES BETWEEN OECD MEMBER COUNTRIES
as at 1st January, 1981

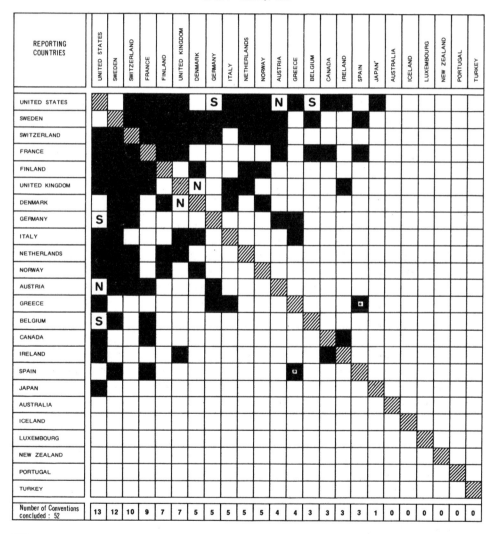

Number of Conventions concluded : 52

Convention in force
Convention signed but not yet in force
} Conventions concluded

N   Negociations proceeding for the establishment of a Convention and conventions initialled

*   Consular convention containing tax provisions

III

PRESENTATION OF THE 1982 ESTATE TAX MODEL

12.   The 1982 Estate Tax Model, the broad lines of which are set out in paragraphs 18 and following, provides a means of settling on a uniform basis the most common problems which arise in the field of international double taxation of estates and inheritances and of gifts. Except for the extension to taxes on gifts *inter vivos,* the new text does not differ appreciably from the previous one as it was not the object of the revision of the 1966 Estate Tax Draft to question its principles and general structures. Those general principles and structures have been applied to taxes on gifts *inter vivos.*

13.   Taxation of estates and inheritances presents problems which have no exact counterpart in income taxation, although there are many analogies between the two. It seemed therefore advisable in 1966 to establish a Draft Convention for estate and inheritance taxes which would constitute a self-contained document with no references to the 1963 Income Tax Draft. The same was true of the Commentaries on the Articles, which only exceptionally contained references from one draft to the other. Nevertheless the Fiscal Committee had, as far as possible, taken as a textual model the Articles and Commentaries which it had prepared for the taxes on income and capital.

14.   In revising the 1966 Estate Tax Draft, the Committee on Fiscal Affairs saw no reason to deviate from that approach. The natural consequence of this is that concepts which are expressed by the same words in both Model Conventions must each be taken to have the same application, due regard being had, wherever appropriate, to the different nature of the forms of taxation in question. Member countries desirous of concluding bilateral conventions applying to both taxes on income and capital, and taxes on estates and inheritances and on gifts, may combine the two Model Conventions.

15.   As in the case of taxes on income and capital it has been the twofold aim of the Committee on Fiscal Affairs to continue to establish a Model Convention which would effectively resolve the double taxation problems that exist among Member countries and which would be acceptable to them all.

16.   During the revision, the Committee on Fiscal Affairs examined in detail many questions of a legal, theoretical or practical character which had been brought to light by the operation of the existing conventions. On a number of points, a wide measure of agreement has made it possible to introduce amplifications to, or changes in, the texts of certain Articles. The essential part of the Committee's work is, however, reflected in the

Commentaries on the Articles, which, in some cases, have been the subject of additions, clarifications or updatings. In other cases, the Committee considered that no purpose would be served by elaborating on the diversity of situations and opinions. Accordingly, the importance and usefulness of the discussions and the work of the Committee on Fiscal Affairs are to be gauged, not merely by the number and nature of the amendments made to the 1966 texts, but also by the numerous exchanges of views and experience in which Government experts engaged and which bear witness to constant international co-operation.

17.   On certain points, because of differences in taxation laws and situations and interests involved, unanimous agreement was not possible. Therefore, either special rules had to be accepted in the 1982 Estate Tax Model, or some States lodged reservations on certain provisions of the Model, as was the case in the 1966 Estate Tax Draft and the 1977 Income Tax Model.

A.   BROAD OUTLINE OF THE MODEL CONVENTION

General

18.   The Model Convention first describes its scope (Chapter I) and defines some terms (Chapter II). The main part is made up of Chapters III and IV, which settle to what extent each of the two Contracting states may tax property and how double taxation is to be eliminated. Then follow the Special Provisions (Chapter V) and the Final Provisions (Chapter VI).

Scope

19.   Most Member countries impose death duties and taxes on gifts *inter vivos* on the value of all the property, wherever it is situated, of a person's estate passing on his death to his heirs, legatees or other beneficiaries, or given by a donor to a donee, if the deceased or the donor, at the time of the death or gift, was domiciled or living permanently within their territory. However, many Member countries impose a comprehensive tax liability also on one or more of other criteria, for example:

  - nationality of the deceased or donor;
  - domicile, residence or nationality of the heir, legatee, donee, etc.; or
  - the fact that either the deceased or donor, or the heir, legatee or donee was, at some prior time, domiciled or resident in their country.

20.   On the other hand most Member countries impose death duties or gift taxes on all or certain property (for example, immovable property) situated in their territory without regard to the domicile, residence or nationality of either the deceased or donor, or the heir, legatee or donee.

21.   As far as the cases described in paragraph 19 above are concerned, the Model Convention follows the course which has already been taken by the 1966 Estate Tax Draft, that is, to restrict the scope of the Convention to estates of, or gifts made by, persons domiciled in one or both Contracting States, thereby disregarding any other criteria which, under the domestic law of a Member country, may lead to a comprehensive tax liability.

22.   Chapter II is intended to catalogue terms which are used in more than one Article of the Convention and which need special definition. Other terms, such as "permanent establishment" and "nationals" are defined in the Articles which deal with these matters.

Taxation of property

23.   For some items of property which form part of the estate of, or of a gift made by, a person domiciled in one Contracting State, a taxation right is given to the other State as the State of *situs* of such property, that is, immovable property falling under Article 5, or permanent establishments or fixed based falling under Article 6 (for the reason given in paragraph 2 of the Commentary on Article 6 the special rule for shipping and aircraft enterprises which appeared in the 1966 Estate Tax Draft has been abandoned in the new Model). Since that taxation is not an exclusive one, the State in which the deceased or donor was domiciled within the meaning of the Convention has to give relief from double taxation by applying either Article 9A or Article 9B (see paragraph 25 below).

24.   For any other property the exclusive taxation right is given to the State of the domicile of the deceased or the donor within the meaning of the Convention. By applying this rule double taxation will also be avoided in cases where both Contracting States impose a comprehensive tax liability for one of the reasons set out in paragraph 19 above since the State which is not the State of domicile within the meaning of the Convention has to exempt property other than that falling under Articles 5 and 6 of the Convention.

25.   Where items of property may be taxed in the State of *situs*, the State of domicile has to choose between the following two methods of eliminating double taxation:

–   the exemption method: property which is taxable in the State of *situs* is then exempted in the State of domicile, but it may be taken into account in determining the rate of tax applicable to the remaining part of the estate or gift;
–   the credit method: property taxable in the State of *situs* is then taxed in the State of domicile, but the tax levied in the State of *situs* is credited against the tax levied by the State of domicile on such property.

26.   The Convention contains further provisions (paragraph 2 of Articles 9A and 9B) for the avoidance of double taxation which may arise by reason of the interconnection which death duties and taxes on gifts *inter vivos* may have in some Member countries under their domestic laws. Furthermore, since most Member countries tax estates, inheritances and gifts on a net basis, detailed provisions as to the attribution of debts are given by the Model Convention (Article 8).

Special provisions

27.   These provisions concern:

–   non-discrimination (Article 10);
–   mutual agreement procedure (Article 11);
–   exchange of information (Article 12);
–   diplomatic agents and consular officers (Article 13);
–   territorial extension (Article 14).

B. GENERAL REMARKS ON THE MODEL CONVENTION

28.   The Committee on Fiscal Affairs has endeavoured, wherever possible, to lay down in each case one single rule. On certain points, however, its was thought necessary to leave in the Convention a certain degree of flexibility compatible with efficient implementation. The most important example of flexibility is Article 9, which allows Member countries a choice between two methods for eliminating double taxation (see paragraph 25 above). Moreover, in some cases, alternative or additional provisions are mentioned in the Commentaries.

Commentaries on the Articles

29.   For each of the Articles in the Convention, there is a detailed Commentary which is designed to illustrate or interpret the provisions. When it revised and updated the texts of the 1966 Estate Tax Draft, the Committee on Fiscal Affairs adopted new explanations as to why new provisions had been inserted in the Article concerned or to clarify the meaning and scope of the provisions of the Article.

30.   As these Commentaries have been drafted and agreed upon by the experts appointed to the Committee on Fiscal Affairs by the governments of Member countries, they are of special importance in the development of international fiscal law. Although the Commentaries are not designed to be annexed in any manner to the conventions to be signed by Member countries, which alone constitute legally-binding international instruments, they can nevertheless be of great assistance in the application of the conventions and, in particular, in the settlement of any disputes.

31.   Observations on the Commentaries have sometimes been inserted at the request of some Member countries who were unable to concur in the interpretation given in the Commentary on the Article concerned. These observations thus do not express any disagreement with the text of the Convention, but furnish a useful indication of the way in which those countries will apply the provisions of the Article in question.

Reservations of certain Member countries

32.   All the Member countries which have participated in establishing the Model Convention are in agreement with its aims and its main provisions. Nevertheless, a certain number of Member countries have entered, on some provisions of the Convention, reservations which are recorded in the Commentaries on the Articles concerned.

33.   The Committee on Fiscal Affairs considers that these reservations must be viewed against the background of the global results which have been obtained. It is understood that insofar as certain Member countries have entered reservations, other Member countries, in negotiating bilateral conventions with the former, will retain their freedom of action in accordance with the principle of reciprocity.

34.   At present, two Member countries (Australia and Canada) do not impose, at Federal level, any taxes on estates or inheritances or on gifts. The Model will therefore have no immediate influence on these countries. Because of its domestic tax legislation regarding estates, inheritances and gifts, Japan is obliged to reserve its position on the Model Convention as a whole.

Relation between the 1966 Estate Tax Draft and the 1982 Estate Tax Model

35.   The Committee on Fiscal Affairs has examined the problem of conflicts of interpretation which could arise as a result of changes in the text of the Articles or of the Commentaries. The Committee considers that existing conventions should, as far as possible, be interpreted in the spirit of the new Commentaries, even though the provisions of existing conventions do not yet contain the more precise wording of the 1982 Estate Tax Model. Member countries wishing to clarify their positions in this respect may do so by means of an exchange of letters between competent authorities in accordance with the mutual agreement procedure. Even in the absence of such an exchange of letters, these authorities would use the mutual agreement procedure to secure this interpretation in particular cases.

Tax avoidance and evasion: improper use of conventions

36.   The Committee on Fiscal Affairs has examined the question of the improper use of double taxation conventions but, in view of the complexity of the problem, it has limited itself, in preparing this Model Convention, to enlarging the Commentary on Article 12 enabling States to exchange information to combat improper use of conventions, tax avoidance and evasion. The Committee is engaged, however, in an in-depth study of problems of abuse or improper use of tax conventions and of ways of dealing with them.

Multilateral convention

37.   The Committee on Fiscal Affairs has considered whether the elaboration and conclusion of a multilateral double taxation convention would be feasible. As in 1966, the Committee has come to the conclusion that, in the present situation, this would meet with great difficulties. It might, however, be possible for certain groups of Member countries to study the possibility of concluding such a convention among themselves on the basis of the Model Convention, subject to certain adaptations they may consider necessary to suit their particular purposes.

IV

CONCLUSIONS

38.   The Committee on Fiscal Affairs suggests that the Council may wish to:

1. recommend Member countries which impose taxes on estates and inheritances or on gifts to pursue their efforts to conclude bilateral conventions for the avoidance of double taxation in respect of such taxes with those Member countries with which they have not yet entered into such conventions and to revise those of the existing conventions between them which may no longer be in keeping with present-day needs;
2. recommend Member countries, when concluding new bilateral conventions or revising existing bilateral conventions between them, to conform to the Model Convention as interpreted by the Commentaries thereto and having regard to the reservations to the Model Convention, which are contained in the present report;
3. request Member countries to notify the Organisation of the text of any new or revised double taxation convention concluded with each other and, where appropriate, of the reasons why the provisions of the Model Convention have not been adopted in such conventions.

39.   The Committee on Fiscal Affairs also suggests that the Council may wish to instruct it to:

1. examine the notifications so supplied and to report to it as appropriate;
2. conduct periodic reviews of situations where double taxation may occur, in the light of experience gained by Member countries, and to make appropriate proposals for its removal.

40.   The Committee on Fiscal Affairs recommends that the present report be published and given appropriate publicity by the OECD Secretariat.

Part II

THE MODEL CONVENTION

SUMMARY OF THE CONVENTION

TITLE AND PREAMBLE

Chapter I

Scope of the Convention

Chapter II

Definitions

Chapter III

Taxing Rules

Chapter IV

Methods for Eliminating Double Taxation

Chapter V

Special Provisions

Chapter VI

Final Provisions

TERMINAL CLAUSE

TITLE OF THE CONVENTION

**Convention between (State A) and (State B)
for the avoidance of double taxation
with respect to taxes on
estates and inheritances and on gifts.**

PREAMBLE OF THE CONVENTION

Note: The Preamble of the Convention shall be drafted in accordance with the constitutional procedure of both Contracting States.

Chapter I

SCOPE OF THE CONVENTION

Article 1

ESTATES, INHERITANCES AND GIFTS COVERED

This Convention shall apply:

a) to estates and inheritances where the deceased was domiciled, at the time of his death, in one or both of the Contracting States, and

b) to gifts where the donor was domiciled, at the time of the gift, in one or both of the Contracting States.

Article 2

TAXES COVERED

1.   This Convention shall apply to taxes on estates and inheritances and on gifts imposed on behalf of a Contracting State or of its political subdivisions or local authorities, irrespective of the manner in which they are levied.

2.   There shall be regarded as taxes on estates and inheritances taxes imposed by reason of death in the form of taxes on the *corpus* of the estate, of taxes on inheritances, of transfer duties, or of taxes on *donationes mortis causa*. There shall be regarded as taxes on gifts taxes imposed on transfers *inter vivos* only because such transfers are made for no, or less than full, consideration.

3.   The existing taxes to which the Convention shall apply are:

a)   (in State A)   ....

b)   (In State B)   ....

4.   The Convention shall apply also to any identical or substantially similar taxes which are imposed after the date of signature of the Convention in addition to, or in place of, the existing taxes. At the end of each year, the competent authorities of the Contracting States shall notify each other of changes which have been made in their respective taxation laws.

Chapter II

DEFINITIONS

Article 3

GENERAL DEFINITIONS

1.   For the purposes of this Convention, unless the context otherwise requires:

a)   the term "property which forms part of the estate of, or of a gift made by, a person domiciled in a Contracting State" includes any property the devolution or transfer of which, under the law of a Contracting State, is liable to a tax covered by the Convention;

b)   the term "competent authority" means:

i)   (in State A) ....

ii)   (in State B) ....

2.   As regards the application of the Convention by a Contracting State, any term not defined therein shall, unless the context otherwise requires, have the meaning which it has under the law of that State concerning the taxes to which the Convention applies.

Article 4

FISCAL DOMICILE

1.   For the purposes of this Convention, the term "person domiciled in a Contracting State" means any person whose estate or whose gift, under the law of that State, is liable to tax therein by reason of the domicile, residence or place of management of that person or any other criterion of a similar nature. However, this term does not include any person whose estate or whose gift is liable to tax in that State only in respect of property situated therein.

2.   Where by reason of the provisions of paragraph 1 an individual is domiciled in both Contracting States, then his status shall be determined as follows:

a)   he shall be deemed to be domiciled in the State in which he has a permanent home available to him; if he has a permanent home available to him in both States, he shall be deemed to be domiciled in the State with which his personal and economic relations are closer (centre of vital interests);

b) if the State in which he has his centre of vital interests cannot be determined, or if he has not a permanent home available to him in either State, he shall be deemed to be domiciled in the State in which he has an habitual abode;

c) if he has an habitual abode in both States or in neither of them, he shall be deemed to be domiciled in the State of which he is a national;

d) if he is a national of both States or of neither of them, the competent authorities of the Contracting States shall settle the question by mutual agreement.

3.   Where by reason of the provisions of paragraph 1 a person other than an individual is domiciled in both Contracting States, then it shall be deemed to be domiciled in the State in which its place of effective management is situated.

Chapter III

TAXING RULES

Article 5

IMMOVABLE PROPERTY

1.   Immovable property which forms part of the estate of, or of a gift made by, a person domiciled in a Contracting State and which is situated in the other Contracting State may be taxed in that other State.

2.   The term "immovable property" shall have the meaning which it has under the law of the Contracting State in which the property in question is situated. The term shall in any case include property accessory to immovable property, livestock and equipment used in agriculture and forestry, rights to which the provisions of general law respecting landed property apply, usufruct of immovable property and rights to variable or fixed payments as consideration for the working of, or the right to work, mineral deposits, sources and other natural resources; ships, boats and aircraft shall not be regarded as immovable property.

3.   The provisions of paragraph 1 shall also apply to immovable property of an enterprise and to immovable property used for the performance of professional services or other activities of an independent character.

Article 6

MOVABLE PROPERTY OF A PERMANENT ESTABLISHMENT
OR A FIXED BASE

1.   Movable property of an enterprise which forms part of the estate of, or of a gift made by, a person domiciled in a Contracting State, which is the business property of a permanent establishment situated in the other Contracting State, may be taxed in that other State.

2.   For the purposes of this Convention, the term "permanent establishment" means a fixed place of business through which the business of an enterprise is wholly or partly carried on.

3.　　The term "permanent establishment" includes especially:

　　a)　a place of management;
　　b)　a branch;
　　c)　an office;
　　d)　a factory;
　　e)　a workshop; and
　　f)　a mine, an oil or gas well, a quarry or any other place of extraction of natural resources.

4.　　A building site or construction or installation project constitutes a permanent establishment only if it lasts more than twelve months.

5.　　Notwithstanding the preceding provisions of this Article, the term "permanent establishment" shall be deemed not to include:

　　a)　the use of facilities solely for the purpose of storage, display or delivery of goods or merchandise belonging to the enterprise;
　　b)　the maintenance of a stock of goods or merchandise belonging to the enterprise solely for the purpose of storage, display or delivery;
　　c)　the maintenance of a stock of goods or merchandise belonging to the enterprise solely for the purpose of processing by another enterprise;
　　d)　the maintenance of a fixed place of business solely for the purpose of purchasing goods or merchandise, or of collecting information, for the enterprise;
　　e)　the maintenance of a fixed place of business solely for the purpose of carrying on for the enterprise any other activity of a preparatory or auxiliary character; or
　　f)　the maintenance of a fixed place of business solely for any combination of activities mentioned in subparagraphs *a)* to *e)*, provided that the overall activity of the fixed place of business resulting from this combination is of a preparatory or auxiliary character.

6.　　Movable property which forms part of the estate of, or of a gift made by, a person domiciled in a Contracting State, used for the performance of professional services or other activities of an independent character and pertaining to a fixed base situated in the other Contracting State, may be taxed in that other State.

Article 7

OTHER PROPERTY

Property, wherever situated, which forms part of the estate of, or of a gift made by, a person domiciled in a Contracting State, and not dealt with in Articles 5 and 6, shall be taxable only in that State.

Article 8

DEDUCTION OF DEBTS

1.   Debts especially secured on any property referred to in Article 5 shall be deducted from the value of that property. Debts, not being especially secured on any property referred to in Article 5, which are represented by the acquisition, conversion, repair or upkeep of any such property, shall be deducted from the value of that property.

2.   Subject to the provisions of paragraph 1, debts pertaining to a permanent establishment referred to in paragraph 1 of Article 6, or to a fixed base referred to in paragraph 6 of Article 6, shall be deducted from the value of the permanent establishment or the fixed base as the case may be.

3.   Other debts shall be deducted from the value of property to which the provisions of Article 7 apply.

4.   If a debt exceeds the value of the property from which it is deductible in a Contracting State, according to the provisions of paragraphs 1 or 2, the excess shall be deducted from the value of any other property taxable in that State.

5.   Any excess still remaining in one Contracting State after the deductions referred to in paragraphs 3 or 4 shall be deducted from the value of the property liable to tax in the other Contracting State.

6.   Where the provisions of paragraphs 1 to 5 would oblige one Contracting State to deduct debts to an extent greater than that provided for under its law, those provisions shall apply only to the extent that the other Contracting State is not obliged to deduct the same debts under its own law.

Chapter IV

METHODS FOR ELIMINATING DOUBLE TAXATION

Article 9A

EXEMPTION METHOD

1.   The Contracting State in which the deceased was domiciled at his death, or the donor was domiciled at the time of the gift, shall exempt from tax any property which, in relation to the same event and in accordance with the provisions of this Convention, may be taxed in the other Contracting State.

2.   The former Contracting State shall also exempt from tax any property which, in relation to a previous gift and in accordance with the provisions of the Convention, may have been taxed in the other Contracting State. That former State, however, shall not exempt from tax any property which was taxable in that State in accordance with the provisions of Articles 5 or 6 of the Convention.

3.   In each case the former Contracting State may take the exempted property into account in calculating the amount of tax on any remaining property.

Article 9B

CREDIT METHOD

1.   The Contracting State in which the deceased was domiciled at his death, or the donor was domiciled at the time of the gift, shall allow as a deduction from the tax calculated according to its law an amount equal to the tax paid in the other Contracting State on any property which, in relation to the same event and in accordance with the provisions of this Convention, may be taxed in that other State.

2.   The former Contracting State shall also allow as a deduction from such tax an amount equal to the tax which has been paid in the other Contracting State on a previous gift in accordance with the provisions of the Convention to the extent that such a deduction has not been allowed under the provisions of paragraph 1 at the time of that gift. That former State, however, shall not allow a deduction in respect of tax paid on property which was taxable in that State in accordance with the provisions of Articles 5 or 6 of the Convention.

3.   The deductions referred to in paragraphs 1 and 2 shall not, however, exceed that part of the tax of the former Contracting State, as computed before any deduction is made, which is attributable to the property in respect of which the deduction is to be allowed.

Chapter V

SPECIAL PROVISIONS

Article 10

NON-DISCRIMINATION

1.   Nationals of a Contracting State, wherever they are domiciled, shall not be subjected in the other Contracting State to any taxation, or any requirement connected therewith, which is other or more burdensome than the taxation and connected requirements to which nationals of that other State in the same circumstances are or may be subjected.

2.   The term "nationals" means:

   a)   all individuals possessing the nationality of a Contracting State;

   b)   all legal persons, partnerships and associations deriving their status as such from the law in force in a Contracting State.

3.   Stateless persons who are domiciled in a Contracting State shall not be subjected in either Contracting State to any taxation, or any requirement connected therewith, which is other or more burdensome than the taxation and connected requirements to which nationals of the State concerned in the same circumstances are or may be subjected.

4.   The provisions of this Article shall, notwithstanding the provisions of Article 2, apply to taxes of every kind and description.

Article 11

MUTUAL AGREEMENT PROCEDUF

1.   Where a person considers that the actions of one or both of the Contracting States result or will result for him in taxation not in accordance with the provisions of this Convention, he may, irrespective of the remedies provided by the domestic laws of those States, present his case to the competent authority of either Contracting State. The case must be presented within three years from the first notification of the action resulting in taxation not in accordance with the provisions of the Convention.

2.   The competent authority, if the objection appears to it to be justified and if it is not itself able to arrive at a satisfactory solution, shall endeavour to resolve the case by mutual agreement with the competent authority of the other Contracting State, with a view to the avoidance of taxation which is not in accordance with the provisions of the Convention. Any agreement reached shall be implemented notwithstanding any time limits in the domestic laws of the Contracting States.

3.　　The competent authorities of the Contracting States shall endeavour to resolve by mutual agreement any difficulties or doubts arising as to the interpretation or application of the Convention. They may also consult together for the elimination of double taxation in cases not provided for in the Convention.

4.　　The competent authorities of the Contracting States may communicate with each other directly for the purpose of reaching an agreement in the sense of the preceding paragraphs. When it seems advisable in order to reach agreement to have an oral exchange of opinions, such exchange may take place through a Commission consisting of representatives of the competent authorities of the Contracting States.

Article 12

EXCHANGE OF INFORMATION

1.　　The competent authorities of the Contracting States shall exchange such information as is necessary for carrying out the provisions of this Convention or of the domestic laws of the Contracting States concerning taxes covered by the Convention insofar as the taxation thereunder is not contrary to the Convention. The exchange of information is not restricted by Article 1. Any information received by a Contracting State shall be treated as secret in the same manner as information obtained under the domestic laws of that State and shall be disclosed only to persons or authorities (including courts and administrative bodies) involved in the assessment or collection of, the enforcement or prosecution in respect of, or the determination of appeals in relation to, the taxes covered by the Convention. Such persons or authorities shall use the information only for such purposes. They may disclose the information in public court proceedings or in judicial decisions.

2.　　In no case shall the provisions of paragraph 1 be construed so as to impose on a Contracting State the obligation:

     a) to carry out administrative measures at variance with the laws or administrative practice of that or of the other State;

     b) to supply information which is not obtainable under the laws, or in the normal course of the administration, of that or of the other State;

     c) to supply information which would disclose any trade, business, industrial, commercial or professional secret or trade process, or information, the disclosure of which would be contrary to public policy (ordre public).

Article 13

DIPLOMATIC AGENTS AND CONSULAR OFFICERS

Nothing in this Convention shall affect the fiscal privileges of diplomatic agents or consular officers under the general rules of international law or under the provisions of special agreements.

Article 14
TERRITORIAL EXTENSION

1.   This Convention may be extended, either in its entirety or with any necessary modifications, [to any part of the territory of (State A) or of (State B) which is specifically excluded from the application of the Convention or] to any State or territory for whose international relations (State A) or (State B) is responsible, which imposes taxes substantially similar in character to those to which the Convention applies. Any such extension shall take effect from such date and subject to such modifications and conditions, including conditions as to termination, as may be specified and agreed between the Contracting States in notes to be exchanged through diplomatic channels or in any other manner in accordance with their constitutional procedures.

2.   Unless otherwise agreed by both Contracting States, the termination of the Convention by one of them under Article 16 shall also terminate, in the manner provided for in that Article, the application of the Convention [to any part of the territory of (State A) or of (State B) or] to any State or territory to which it has been extended under this Article.

Note: The words between square brackets are of relevance when, by special provision, a part of the territory of a Contracting State is excluded from the application of the Convention.

Chapter VI

FINAL PROVISIONS

Article 15

ENTRY INTO FORCE

1.   This Convention shall be ratified and the instruments of ratification shall be exchanged at .... as soon as possible.

2.   The Convention shall enter into force upon the exchange of instruments of ratification and its provisions shall have effect:

    a)   (in State A) ....

    b)   (in State B) ....

Article 16

TERMINATION

    This Convention shall remain in force until terminated by a Contracting State. Either Contracting State may terminate the Convention, through diplomatic channels, by giving notice of termination at least six months before the end of any calendar year after the year .... In such event, the Convention shall cease to have effect:

    a)   (in State A) ....

    b)   (In State B) ....

TERMINAL CLAUSE

Note: The terminal clause shall be drafted in accordance with the constitutional procedure of both Contracting States.

Part III

COMMENTARY ON THE MODEL CONVENTION

COMMENTARY ON ARTICLE 1
CONCERNING ESTATES, INHERITANCES AND GIFTS COVERED BY THE CONVENTION

I. COMMENTARY ON THE PROVISIONS OF THE ARTICLE

1.   Article 1 establishes the scope of the Convention as to the transfers of property covered by its provisions. Whereas certain of the older estate tax conventions limit their scope to estates of nationals of one of the States, most recent conventions like the 1966 Estate Tax Draft apply to estates of deceased persons who were domiciled in one or both of the Contracting States. Some conventions have a wider scope in that they apply to taxpayers of the Contracting States: they are therefore applicable to persons who, although not domiciled nor residing in either State, are nevertheless liable to tax in each of them. Most Member countries take the view that it is preferable to limit the scope of a double taxation convention by reference to property of persons who are either domiciled in, or are residents of, one or both of the Contracting States. It is considered that, by taking part in the economic life of the State where he has settled, although not possessing its nationality, and by contributing to the public expenditure there like a citizen of the country, the deceased will normally have become sufficiently integrated in the community for it to be proper for him and his heirs to benefit from any international conventions for the avoidance of double taxation which may be concluded by his State of domicile. This Model Convention has been drawn up on this basic principle: subparagraph *a)* therefore provides that the Convention shall apply to estates and inheritances where the deceased was domiciled in one or both of the Contracting States at the time of his death.

2.   Since this Convention also covers gift taxes (see paragraph 2 of the Commentary on Article 2), the same principle has been adopted in subparagraph *b)* in relation to the domicile of the donor.

3.   The question of domicile is dealt with in Article 4.

4.   The principle set out in the Article has been adopted because most Member countries, including those with inheritance taxes, tax the total estate or gift wherever the property is situated, that is, they impose a comprehensive tax liability if the deceased or the donor was domiciled in their country.

5.   However, some Member countries also impose a comprehensive tax liability where:

   a)   the deceased or the donor, although not in fact living there, is a national thereof;

   b)   the heir, legatee, beneficiary or donee is either a national thereof or is domiciled there (even if the deceased or the donor was not so domiciled); or

c) the deceased or the donor, or the heir, legatee, beneficiary or donee, is deemed to retain his domicile there for a certain period after he has transferred his real domicile to another State (the so-called "extended domicile").

6.   Where two Contracting States each impose tax and in one of them (the first State) the tax is imposed in the circumstances referred to in paragraph 5 above, the Model Convention will cover the cases of double taxation if:

a)   the deceased or the donor is domiciled within the meaning of the Convention in the other Contracting State; or

b)   the deceased or the donor is domiciled within the meaning of the Convention in a third State which has concluded a convention on the lines of this Model with the first State.

The following examples illustrate the situation.

7.   *EXAMPLE 1*

The deceased was a national of Sate A, but lived for the last 15 years exclusively in State B. His estate includes property falling under Article 7. If both States tax the total estate, State A by reason of the nationality of the deceased and State B by reason of his residence, there is a double taxation. The Convention applies, since the deceased was domiciled within the meaning of the Convention in one of the Contracting States, that is, State B. Under Article 7, the sole taxation right in respect of that property belongs to State B, the State of the deceased's domicile. State A may no longer excercise its taxation right based solely on the nationality of the deceased.

8.   *EXAMPLE 2*

The deceased was domiciled in State A. His sole heir is domiciled in State B. The estate includes property falling under Article 7. If both States tax the total estate, State A by reason of the domicile of the deceased and State B by reason of the domicile of the heir, there is a double taxation. The convention applies, since the deceased was domiciled in one of the Contracting States, that is State A. Under Article 7, the sole taxation right in respect of that property belongs to State A, the State of the deceased's domicile. State B may no longer exercise its taxation right based solely on the domicile of the heir.

9.   *EXAMPLE 3*

The deceased was a national of State A, but lived for the last 15 years exclusively in State B. His estate includes immovable property situated in State C.

a)   *First double taxation* (States A and C)

If State A taxes the total estate by reason of the nationality of the deceased and State C taxes the immovable property situated in its territory, there is a double taxation in respect of that property. The convention between States A and C does not apply, since the deceased was not domiciled within the meaning of the Convention in one of the Contracting States but in State B.

b)   *Second double taxation* (States A and B)

Both States tax the total estate, including the immovable property situated in State C, State A by reason of the nationality of the deceased and State B by reason of his residence. The convention between States A and B applies, since the deceased was domiciled within the meaning of the Convention in one of the Contracting States, that is, State B. Under that convention, the immovable property situated in State C, which is, for the two Contracting States, a third State, is to be treated as property falling under Article 7. The case is therefore similar to Example 1. The sole taxation right belongs to State B as the State of the deceased's domicile. State A may no longer exercise its taxation right based solely on the nationality of the deceased. Since State A has to give up its taxation right, the first double taxation, which could not be avoided by the convention between States A and C, is avoided by the operation of the convention between States A and B.

c) *Third double taxation* (States B and C)

Both States tax the immovable property, State B by reason of the residence of the deceased and State C by reason of the situation of the property. The convention between States B and C applies, since the deceased, by reason of his residence, was domiciled within the meaning of the Convention in one of the Contracting States, that is, State B. State C has a taxation right as the country of *situs* (see Article 5) and State B has to give relief under Articles 9A or 9B for the tax of State C.

10.   *EXAMPLE 4*

The deceased was domiciled in State A. His sole heir is domiciled in State B. The estate includes immovable property situated in State C.

a) *First double taxation* (States B and C)

If State B taxes the total estate by reason of the domicile of the heir and State C taxes the immovable property situated in its territory, there is a double taxation in respect of that property. The convention between States B and C does not apply, since the deceased was not domiciled within the meaning of the Convention in one of the Contracting States but in State A.

b) *Second double taxation* (States A and B)

Both States tax the total estate, including the immovable property situated in State C, State A by reason of the domicile of the deceased and State B by reason of the domicile of the heir. The convention between States A and B applies, since the deceased was domiciled within the meaning of the Convention in one of the Contracting States, that is, State A. Under that convention, the immovable property situated in State C, which is, for the two Contracting States, a third State, is to be treated as property falling under Article 7. The case is therefore similar to Example 2. The sole taxation right belongs to State A as the State of the deceased's domicile. State B may no longer exercise its taxation right based solely on the domicile of the heir. Since State B has to give up its taxation right, the first double taxation, which could not be avoided by the convention between States B and C, is avoided by the operation of the convention between States A and B.

c) *Third double taxation* (States A and C)

Both States tax the immovable property, State A by reason of the domicile of the deceased and State C by reason of the situation of the property. The convention between States A and C applies, since the deceased was domiciled in one of the Contracting States, that is, State A. State C has a taxation right as the country of *situs* (see Article 5) and State A has to give relief under Articles 9A or 9B for the tax of State C.

11.   The same reasoning shall apply to more complicated cases, for example, where the deceased, a national of State A but domiciled in State B, leaves property situated in State C to an heir, a national of State D, but domiciled in State E. If all of these States have concluded among themselves bilateral conventions along the lines of this Model, the result is that States A, D and E lose their taxation rights (under their conventions with State B), State C may tax as the country of *situs* and State B has to give relief under Articles 9A or 9B for the tax of State C.

12.   Where, in the circumstances mentioned in paragraph 5, the deceased was not domiciled in either Contracting State, and those States have not concluded conventions with the State of the deceased's domicile, unrelieved double taxation will remain. The Committee on Fiscal Affairs decided not to include such residual cases within the scope of the Model Convention, since such forms of tax liability are found only in a few Member countries. Moreover, in the rare practical cases, double taxation will often be avoided by the unilateral reliefs provided in the countries concerned. Finally, where double taxation does occur, it will be avoided where Member countries adhere to the Council's Recommendation and conclude double taxation conventions on the basis of this Model. Accordingly, as the network of double taxation conventions among Member countries becomes more widespread, unrelieved double taxation will become progressively more rare. There seemed therefore to be no need to enlarge the Convention to cover such special cases.

13.   Although the Article contains what could be called the "personal scope" of the Convention, it should be stressed that it does not apply to "persons" but to estates of, or gifts made by, persons domiciled in one or both of the Contracting States. The Convention applies to such estates or gifts regardless of who pays or bears the tax. The Convention is therefore applicable where the deceased or the donor, domiciled in one Contracting State, leaves or gives property situated in the other State even if one of the two States imposes a tax on the *corpus* of an estate or a gift tax on the donor, and the other State imposes an inheritance tax on the heirs or legatees, or a gift tax on the donee.

II. SPECIAL FEATURES OF THE DOMESTIC LAW OF CERTAIN MEMBER COUNTRIES

14.   Under the laws of most countries arrangements can be made by which the ownership rights in property can be split, thus enabling the right to enjoy the benefits of property to devolve or to be transferred according to the wishes of the original owner or of the persons designated by him without any change of formal legal ownership. The arrangements available vary from country to country. In countries whose legal system is based on English "common law", trusts are frequently established. In others a usufruct, *fideicommissum* or substitute *fideicommissum* may be established or a foundation created. Since in a number of Member countries special taxation rules exist to deal with these arrangements, it is desirable that a double taxation convention should also cover these rules. In some cases the Convention will apply automatically and in others it may need adaptation. The following paragraphs outline the problems that may arise in bilateral negotiations and indicate possible approaches to them.

A. Trusts

15.   In those countries whose legal system is based on English common law a trust may be established either by a gift *inter vivos* or under the terms of a will. A trust exists when one person, the "trustee", who is the "legal" owner of property, holds the property under a legally enforceable obligation to use it for the benefit of another person or group of persons, the "beneficiary" or "beneficiaries", who are the "beneficial" owners of the property. A trust generally is created when one person, the "settlor", transfers property to a designated trustee (or trustees), with directions that the trustee exercises control over the property in a particular way for the benefit of the beneficiaries.

16.   Trusts can be classified into three categories according to the directions given to the trustee:

    a)   trusts where the beneficiary has an immediate right to the whole of the income and capital of the trust – called "bare" trusts;

    b)   trusts where an identified beneficiary or beneficiaries have a right only to the whole or part of the income or enjoyment of the property but not the capital – called "interest in possession" trusts; and

    c)   trusts where the instrument does not specify the rights of the potential beneficiary or beneficiaries, the trustee being given discretion as to whether, how, when or for whose benefit property or income is to be distributed – called "discretionary" trusts.

17.   Bare trusts are not unlike nominee holdings and the beneficiary is treated, for tax purposes, as the real owner. Therefore, the Convention will apply in the same way as it does to any other property.

18.   In the case of an "interest in possession" trust or a "discretionary" trust, its creation, whether by gift *inter vivos* or on death, will be covered by the Convention if the settlor (that is, the donor or the deceased person) is domiciled in one of the Contracting States. Some States also impose tax upon events occurring subsequent to the creation of the trust. This tax prevents the beneficial enjoyment of property from passing from one person to another or from one generation to another without a tax charge being incurred: under general law there is no identifiable gift or property forming part of the estate of a deceased person. These charges seek to ensure a broad parity of treatment between property held directly and property held in trust.

19.   The following examples illustrate how trusts can be used to pass on the beneficial enjoyment of property without any change in the legal ownership which remains with the trustee:

    a)   X transfers property to a trustee to be held in trust, with the income from the property payable to Y for life; upon Y's death, the income is to be paid for life to Z, Y's wife; upon Z's death the property is to be distributed absolutely to U, Z's child. During the existence of the trust, the trustee is the legal owner of the property, the beneficial enjoyment of which will belong successively to Y, Z and U. The trustee is not free to accumulate income and he has no discretion as to whom the property is eventually given;

    b)   X transfers property to a trustee, to be held in trust for X's children or grandchildren. The trustee is empowered to accumulate the income or to distribute it among the beneficiaries or to distribute the capital as is necessary for the maintenance or well-being of any beneficiary. Upon the death of the surviving child, any remaining property is to be distributed outright to the surviving grandchildren. During the existence of the trust, the trustee is the legal owner of the property. In this instance the trustee is given a wide measure of discretion as to how the income and the capital of the trust is to be used. A trust of this type would be called a discretionary trust. The children and the grandchildren to whom or for whose benefit the income and capital of the trust is applied would not be regarded as having interests in possession although they may have enjoyed the use of the property.

The net effect of the arrangements in each example is to transfer the benefit of the property from one person to another or from one generation to another without giving rise to an estate, inheritance or gift tax charge. These arrangements provide a major means of mitigating the impact of wealth transfer taxes, particularly in common law countries where holding property in trust is a familiar practice.

20.   The way in which Member countries, whose law is based upon English common law, deal with trusts for tax purposes varies considerably. In general however, as far as interest in possession trusts are concerned, they will frequently impose tax when the interest in possession of a beneficiary comes to an end, for example, when the beneficiaries change. While it is even more difficult to generalise in the case of discretionary trusts, tax will usually be charged where property is distributed from the trust; in the case of the United States, however, there is a charge only when the distribution has the effect of transmitting wealth from one generation to another. The United Kingdom, in addition to the charge on distributions, also imposes charges at periodic intervals during the existence of the trust.

B.   Foundations

21.   Foundations are normally set up as legal persons. Property is transferred by the "founder" to that legal person on terms which create an obligation on the part of the administrator of the foundation to use the property for purposes stipulated by the founder. The use of the property for such purposes may be stipulated by the founder in more or less certain terms or may be left to the discretion of the administrator. In some ways foundations resemble discretionary trusts, but unlike them, foundations are treated as legal entities. Where the principal beneficiaries of the foundation are the founder himself or persons closely connected with him, some Member countries apply special tax rules disregarding the legal existence of the foundation and treating the property involved as belonging to the founder or to the beneficiaries.

C.   Fideicommissum

22.   A means of disposing of property which bears some resemblance to transferring property to a trust is the creation of a *fideicommissum*. A *fideicommissum* is a disposition either *inter vivos* or on death by the terms of which property is transferred to several persons successively, subject to the condition that a successor nominee be alive at the moment of the death of the preceding nominee. A *fideicommissum* may be also instituted by law. In general, under private law, the successor is deemed to acquire the property from the creator of the *fideicommissum,* but for tax purposes some Member countries may view the property as acquired from the previous beneficiary. A conditional transfer of property is broadly similar to a transfer creating a *fideicommissum.* A conditional transfer would exist, for example, where a person transfers property at death or *inter vivos* to another person subject to the condition that the property, or what is left of it, has to be passed on to another person on the occurrence of a specified event.

23.   The domestic laws of Member countries may differ as to the nature of the legal rights of the different beneficiaries, and also as to whether the property or the residue passing to the ultimate beneficiary is treated as derived from the previous beneficiary or from the original transferor.

D. Usufructs

24.   In Member countries whose law is derived from Roman law a usufruct can be established. A usufruct may be described as a temporary division of ownership rights and may be created by operation of law, by contract (for example, by gift), or by will. The usufructor is given the right to use property, the title to which is vested in another person (the bare-proprietor), and to derive the profits from it. The usufruct normally comes to an end on the death of the usufructor, but it may end on the expiry of a fixed period or on some default by the usufructor. The ending of the usufruct will normally result in the reversion of the full rights of ownership to the bare-proprietor, but in some cases it may lead to the establishment of a new usufruct.

25.   Where property is subject to a usufruct most Member countries will levy death or gift taxes on the following two occasions:

   a)   the transfer of the bare-ownership;
   b)   the establishment of the usufruct.

Some Member countries also levy tax when the usufructor transfers his interest, when the expiry of one usufruct leads to the creation of another or when the ending of the usufruct leads to the restoration of the full ownership of the property in the bare-proprietor.

E.   Possible approaches to the application of the Article

26.   The charges that arise on the setting up of a trust, foundation, *fideicommissum* or usufruct will be covered by Article 1. Difficulties may arise as to the application of the Article to taxable events subsequent to the original transfer of the property. There may be circumstances where, with respect to the same event, Contracting States may identify different persons as the transferor. The most typical cases will arise where tax is imposed upon the termination of a usufruct, upon the succession of a beneficiary under a *fideicommissum,* or upon the transfer of property held in trust, whether an "interest in possession" or a "discretionary" trust. For example, on the termination of a usufruct or an "interest in possession" under a trust, some States may regard the termination as a transfer from the usufructor or the life tenant while others will regard the termination as a transfer from the creator of the usufruct or the trust. Similarly, as regards the taxation of a "discretionary" trust, some States may regard the charge as imposed upon a distribution from the trust while others may regard it as imposed upon a transfer from an intervening beneficiary. Where, in the first case, the usufructor or the life tenant and the original creator, or, in the second case, the trust and the intervening beneficiary, are not both domiciled in either of the Contracting States, a conflict may arise as to whether the Convention applies.

27.   To solve these difficulties the Convention could be made to apply on one of the following bases:

   a)   to a trust, foundation, *fideicommissum* or usufruct created by a person domiciled in one or both of the Contracting States;
   b)   to a trust, foundation, *fideicommissum* or usufruct where the beneficiary, on whose death (or at some other event) tax is imposed, is domiciled in one or both of the Contracting States; or
   c)   to a trust or foundation established under the law of one of the Contracting States.

28. Moreover, the Article may have to be modified to cover charges imposed by some States on events occuring subsequent to the creation of a trust, usufruct, *fideicommissum* or foundation because some States may take the view that the terms "estate" and "gift" are not sufficiently comprehensive to cover such charges (see paragraph 6 of the Commentary on Article 3).

29. Due to the differences in the civil and taxation laws of Member countries, it was not possible to insert in the Convention provisions which would be acceptable to all States. It is easier to decide in bilateral negotiations whether and to what extent two States may need special rules. Contracting States are, therefore, left free to insert special provisions in their bilateral conventions to deal with these problems.

RESERVATIONS ON THE ARTICLE

30. *Belgium* and *Luxembourg* do not tax gifts under their domestic laws on the basis of the domicile of the donor, and reserve their positions on subparagraph b) of the Article. Whilst accepting the criterion of *situs* as far as immovable property is concerned, these countries wish, in accordance with their domestic laws regarding gifts of movable property, to preserve the taxation rights of the State whose law governs the legal title to the transfer of the property (usually an authenticated deed). In bilateral negotiations these countries are prepared to consider the most appropriate means for avoiding any resulting double taxation of gifts.

31. Under the domestic law of *Japan,* the sole criterion of unlimited liability to tax in respect of the acquisition of property by inheritance, legacy or gift is possession by the heir, legatee or donee of domicile in Japan. The domicile of the deceased or donor is completely immaterial. This makes it extremely difficult to reconcile Japan's inheritance and gift tax system with the Model Convention. Consequently, Japan is obliged to reserve its position on the Model Convention as a whole.

32. *Turkey* reserves the right to impose estate, inheritance or gift tax on a residual basis on the entire estate or gifts, wherever located, of Turkish citizens domiciled abroad at the time of death or gift.

33. The *United States* reserves the right to impose estate or gift tax on a residual basis on the entire estate or gifts, wherever located, of United States citizens domiciled abroad at the time of death or gift.

Trusts

34. *Ireland* imposes a comprehensive tax charge where the domicile of the creator of a trust is Irish or where a trust is established under the law of Ireland and reserves the right to apply the Convention to such trusts.

35. The *United Kingdom* reserves the right to extend the scope of the Convention to ensure that it applies to settled property, wherever situated, where the settler was domiciled in the United Kingdom at the time the settlement was made.

COMMENTARY ON ARTICLE 2
CONCERNING TAXES COVERED BY THE CONVENTION

I. PRELIMINARY REMARKS

1.   The Article is intended:

- to make the terminology and nomenclature relating to the taxes covered by the Convention more acceptable and precise;
- to ensure identification of the Contracting States' taxes covered by the Convention;
- to widen as much as possible the field of application of the Convention by including as far as possible, and in harmony with the domestic laws of the Contracting States, the taxes imposed by their political subdivisions or local authorities;
- to avoid the necessity of concluding a new Convention whenever the Contracting States' domestic laws are modified; and
- to provide for the periodic exchange of information about changes which have been made in their respective taxation laws.

2.   The 1966 Estate Tax Draft did not cover taxes on gifts *inter vivos,* although the Commentaries recognised that such taxes were broadly similar to taxes on estates and inheritances, especially where estate tax was payable on gifts made shortly before death. Since 1966 some OECD Member countries have introduced taxes that apply both to gifts *inter vivos* and to property transferred on death. Some other Member countries have integrated gift and estate or inheritance taxes. It has to be recognised that, where gift taxes are imposed in addition to estate or inheritance taxes, anomalies will arise if gifts are not subject to the same rules as transfers on death. Accordingly, on the occasion of the revision of the 1966 Estate Tax Draft, the Committee on Fiscal Affairs came to the conclusion that it was appropriate to include gift taxes within the scope of the new Model. Since a Contracting State may already give double taxation relief to property forming part of an estate or an inheritance, the time may now be ripe for that Contracting State to consider giving such relief to property included in a gift, especially since, in many countries, the taxation of gifts and of estates and inheritances is integrated.

3.   The inclusion of taxes on gifts *inter vivos* within the scope of the Convention in no way affects the deductibility of gifts for income tax purposes.

II. COMMENTARY ON THE PROVISIONS OF THE ARTICLE

Paragraph 1

4.   This paragraph establishes the scope of the Convention as to the taxes covered, namely: taxes on estates and inheritances and taxes on gifts. It is immaterial on behalf of which authorities such taxes are imposed; it may be the State itself or its political subdivisions or local authorities (constituent States, regions, provinces, "départements", cantons, districts, "arrondissements", "Kreise", municipalities or groups of municipalities, etc.). The method of levying the taxes is equally immaterial; they may be levied in the form of taxes or surcharges, or as additional taxes ("centimes additionnnels"), etc.

Paragraph 2

5.   This paragraph gives a definition of taxes on estates and inheritances and of taxes on gifts *inter vivos*. Taxes on estates and inheritances include all taxes which are imposed by reason of death in the form of taxes on the *corpus* of the estate, taxes on inheritances, transfer duties and taxes on *donationes mortis causa*. Moreover, provided that they are taxes which are imposed by reason of death, it is immaterial whether they are imposed on property actually left by the deceased on his death or on property which he transferred during his life-time in such conditions that, under the law of one or both of the Contracting States, the property transferred is subject to estate tax on the death of the transferor. Taxes on gifts *inter vivos* include all taxes which are levied on gifts (other than *mortis causa*) or other gratuitous transfers of property. However, taxes which are imposed on transactions irrespective of whether or not such transactions are made for full consideration, for example, taxes on capital gains on the transfer of immovable property, of securities, of shares or the like, are not regarded as gift taxes for the purposes of this Convention.

6.   Clearly, a State possessing taxing powers – and it alone – may levy the taxes imposed by its legislation together with any duties or charges accessory to them: increases, costs, interest, etc. It has not been considered necessary to specify this in the Article, as it is obvious that, in the levying of the tax, the accessory duties or charges depend on the same rule as the principal tax.

7.   Property which is included in the tax base for death duties in one State and for gift tax in the other State is dealt with in the Commentary on Articles 9A and 9B.

Paragraph 3

8.   This paragraph lists all the taxes in force at the time of signature of the Convention which are covered by that Convention.

Paragraph 4

9.   This paragraph provides that the Convention is also to apply to all identical or substantially similar taxes which are imposed after the date of signature of the Convention in addition to, or in place of, the existing taxes. This provision is necessary to prevent the Convention from becoming inoperative in the event of one of the States modifying its taxation laws.

10.   Each State undertakes to notify to the other any amendments made to its taxation laws, by communicating to it at the end of each year, when necessary, particulars of changes in the existing taxes or of new or substituted taxes imposed during the year.

OBSERVATION ON THE COMMENTARY

11.   *Spain* observes that under Spanish law, some taxes are considered as taxes on estates and inheritances which do not correspond to the concepts used in paragraph 2 of the Article.

RESERVATIONS ON THE ARTICLE

12.   *Spain* and the *United States* reserve their positions on that part of paragraph 1 which states that the Convention should apply to taxes of political subdivisions or local authorities.

COMMENTARY ON ARTICLE 3
CONCERNING GENERAL DEFINITIONS

I. PRELIMINARY REMARKS

1.   This Article groups together the general provisions required for the interpretation of the terms used in the Convention which are deemed to be necessary; where Contracting States agree bilaterally to add to the Convention any further general definitions (for example, a definition of the term "gifts"), those definitions should be inserted in this Article. It should be noted, however, that the meaning of some important terms is explained elsewhere in the Convention. Thus, the term "domicile" is defined in Article 4, while the meaning of certain terms appearing in other Articles ("immovable property", "permanent establishment", "nationals") is clarified by the provisions of those Articles.

2.   In addition to the definitions contained in the Article, Contracting States are free to agree bilaterally on the definition of the terms "a Contracting State" and "the other Contracting State".

3.   The Article gives no definition of the term "person". From the context of the Convention it follows that this term should be read in a very wide sense (see especially paragraph 3 of Article 4) covering all individuals, companies and other entities whose estates or gifts are, under the law of a Contracting State, subject to the taxes covered by the Convention. Contracting States are, however, free to agree in bilateral negotiations upon a definition of the term by using the terminology used in the 1977 OECD Income Tax Model.

4.   Furthermore, the Convention gives no definition of the term "gift", on which the laws of Member countries differ widely. Where, under the domestic law of a Contracting State, a transaction is considered to be a gift, that transaction, subject to the provisions of Article 1, is covered by the Convention and it is irrelevant whether or not the other Contracting State also considers that same transaction to be a gift.

5.   The question whether an activity is performed within the framework of an enterprise or is deemed to constitute in itself an enterprise has always been interpreted according to the provisions of the domestic laws of the Contracting States. No definition, properly speaking, of the term "enterprise" has therefore been attempted in this Article.

II. COMMENTARY ON THE PROVISIONS OF THE ARTICLE

Paragraph 1

6.   The taxing rules provided in Articles 5 to 7 relate to "property which forms part of the estate of, or of a gift made by ...". Taken literally, the words "which forms part of the estate" may be construed as not conferring taxation rights on States which tax not the estate itself but inheritances. Furthermore, there could be some doubts about whether these rules cover taxes on the transfer of property which does not form part of the estate in the strict sense. For example, under the taxation laws of many Member countries, gifts *inter vivos* are subsequently included in the taxation of the estate on death. Finally, certain property held in trust may be subject to tax although not part of an estate or of a gift. The definition given in subparagraph *a)* of paragraph 1 will ensure that all these cases will be covered by the taxing rules of Articles 5 to 7.

7.   The absence of any general definition of the term "competent authority" in subparagraph *b)* of paragraph 1 has regard to the fact that, in some Member countries, the execution of double taxation conventions does not fall exclusively within the competence of the highest tax authorities but that some matters are reserved or may be delegated to other authorities. The present Model, while indicating that the definition is necessary, enables each Contracting State to nominate one or more authorities as being competent.

Paragraph 2

8.   This paragraph provides a general rule of interpretation in respect of terms used in the Convention but not defined therein.

COMMENTARY ON ARTICLE 4
CONCERNING FISCAL DOMICILE

I. PRELIMINARY REMARKS

1.   Article 4 defines the term "person domiciled in a Contracting State"; the definition is similar to the term "resident of a Contracting State" which is used in the 1977 Income Tax Model. Although it was felt desirable that the wording should be similar, "domiciled in" has been used instead of "resident of" as this was the term used in the 1966 Estate Tax Draft. In some Member countries estate and gift taxes are based on "residence" and, for them, "residence" has virtually the same meaning as "domicile". In others, especially those whose legal system is based on English common law, these taxes are based on "domicile" which in those countries has a different meaning from residence, domicile denoting a more lasting connection with the country concerned.

2.   The concept of "a person domiciled in a Contracting State" has various functions and is of importance in three cases:

    a)   in determing the estates, inheritances and gifts to which the Convention applies;
    b)   in solving cases where double taxation arises in consequence of the double domicile of the same person; and
    c)   in solving cases where double taxation arises as a consequence of taxation in the State of domicile and in the State of *situs*.

3.   The Article defines the term "person domiciled in a Contracting State" and is intended to solve cases of conflict where both States consider a given person to be domiciled in their territory. The Article is not intended to resolve the conflict which may arise where States consider a transfer to have been made by different persons (see paragraph 26 of the Commentary on Article 1).

4.   Generally, under their domestic laws, States tax property wherever it is situated, that is, they impose a comprehensive tax liability, if the deceased or the donor was domiciled or resident there. Where domicile is used as a basis for imposing tax the term does not necessarily have the same meaning as it has in general law. Where residence, habitual abode or any other similar criterion is used, a comprehensive liability may arise on the estates of, or on gifts made by, persons who stay continually, or in some cases for a limited period only, in the territory of the State.

5.   Double taxation conventions do not normally provide a common definition of "domicile" but leave this to be determined in accordance with the domestic laws of each Contracting State. They do not therefore lay down standards which the provisions of the domestic laws on "domicile" have to fulfill in order that claims for comprehensive tax liability can be accepted between Contracting States. This Model follows the same approach and does not specify the conditions under which the estate or gift of a person is subject to a comprehensive tax liability in either Contracting State.

6.   This manifests itself quite clearly in the cases where there is no conflict between two domiciles, but where the conflict exists only between domicile and situs. However, the same view applies in conflicts between two domiciles. The special point in these cases is only that no solution of the conflict can be arrived at by reference to the concept of domicile adopted in the domestic laws of the States concerned. In these cases special provisions must be established in the Convention to determine which of the two concepts of domicile is to be given preference. The following examples illustrate how these rules work.

7.   *EXAMPLE 1*

A person who from his birth had been domiciled in State A accepted employment in State B. Without retaining a home in State A, he settled with his wife and children in State B where he rented a house and took his furniture, etc. Supposing that, according to the domestic laws, he is regarded as being domiciled at his death in both States, then this conflict of laws must be resolved by the Convention. In this particular case, paragraph 2 of the Article gives preference to State B where the deceased's only permanent home was.

8.   *EXAMPLE 2*

A person possessed in State A a permanent home where he lived with his wife and children. At his death, however, he was making a temporary stay, without his wife and children, in State B, to carry out some work there, either on behalf of an enterprise or on his own account. For this purpose he had stayed at a hotel or at a lodging obtained for him by his employer. Supposing that, according to the domestic laws, he is regarded as being domiciled at his death in both States, paragraph 2 of the Article gives preference to State A because his only permanent home was in that State.

9.   *EXAMPLE 3*

A single person, who carried on a business in State A, had a permanent home in that State. He also possessed in State B another place of abode for his exclusive use where he stayed periodically. Supposing that, according to the domestic laws, he is regarded as being domiciled at his death in both States, paragraph 2 of the Article gives preference to State A because the deceased's centre of vital interests was in that State.

A.   Domicile of dependency

10.   The special rules in paragraph 2 of the Article are used to resolve all conflicts of domicile whatever the basis of the claim to domicile in either country. In particular, these rules apply to persons to whom the ordinary law has attributed a domicile of dependency (that is, where under the domestic law of a State the domicile of one person is determined by the domicile of another, for example, where a wife or minor children are deemed to have the domicile of the husband or parent). In such cases the domicile of dependency will be disregarded if it does not agree with the circumstances of the deceased person. Thus, a husband and wife who are estranged live entirely apart; the husband is domiciled in State A; the wife has her permanent home in State B; in the event of the death of the wife, preference is given to State B.

B.   Domicile of origin

11.   Under the laws of some States the deceased is deemed to have died domiciled in the State by reason that the law attributes to him a domicile of origin there. By "domicile

of origin" is meant the domicile which the deceased acquired at birth and which he is deemed to have retained for the rest of his life, unless it can be shown that he had clearly abandoned all his connections with his country of origin, that he had no intention of reviving them again at a later date and that he had settled permanently elsewhere. Where, according to the law of one of these States, the deceased still had his domicile of origin there at his death, and the other Contracting State also considers that the deceased was domiciled in its territory, then the conflict between the two domiciles must be resolved according to the special rules in paragraph 2 of the Article. In such cases, the domicile of origin will be disregarded if it does not agree with the circumstances of the deceased person. Thus, States which claim their taxation rights on the basis of "domicile of origin" may have to cede their primary taxation rights under paragraph 2 in cases where a person has recently established a residence in another Contracting State. It is, however, to be noted that, on the other hand, such States cannot make use of the taxation right conferred on them by the Convention to tax on the basis of domicile a person who resides in their territory without forming a firm intention of residing there permanently because, under their domestic law, such a person would not be regarded as having acquired a domicile there. States which want to provide greater reciprocity are free to do so in bilateral negotiations.

C.   Extended domicile (nationality)

12.   Certain Member countries have expressed some apprehension lest, as a result of the superseding of the domestic law by Article 4, some people should resort to a form of tax avoidance in which, for instance – in contemplation of their death – they transfer their home or place of habitual abode from the State where they had always lived to another State without, however, abandoning their connections with the first State. This form of tax avoidance is countered in those States whose law imposes tax on the total estate of a national even if he was domiciled abroad. As indicated in the Commentaries on Article 7 (see paragraphs 5 to 7) and on Articles 9A and 9B (see paragraphs 70 *et seq.*), the possibility is afforded to such States of taxing the estate of a national if he had been domiciled in his State of nationality within, for example, ten years preceding his death; this right to tax, however, is merely subsidiary to the right to tax of the State in which the deceased is deemed to have died domiciled according to Article 4. Analogously, it is open to Contracting States whose law does not impose tax on the basis of nationality to stipulate by bilateral agreement that in the case of a person who, according to the domestic laws, died domiciled in both States, that State which, by Article 4, is not to be considered as the State of domicile may – if the person died a national of that State but not of the other and had been domiciled in the first State within the meaning of Article 4 at any time within ten years preceding death – tax the total estate according to its domestic law. This taxation right will be subsidiary to the right to tax of the other State considered by the Convention as the State of domicile. The subsidiary character of this taxation right implies that the first State – the one not considered by the Convention as the State of domicile – must give credit, not only for any tax levied by other countries on the basis of *situs,* but also for the tax levied by the other Contracting State (the one which by the Convention is to be considered as the State of domicile). The same principles apply in the case of gifts. The provision proposed in paragraph 73 of the Commentary on Articles 9A and 9B may serve as a model in this case also.

D. Persons present in a State for a temporary purpose

13. Special problems may arise in respect of a person who is domiciled in one of the States and is resident, and therefore domiciled for the purposes of Article 4, in the other State, but who does not intend to remain permanently in that other State. Such a case would arise where an executive of an international company is assigned to work for a certain period outside his own country. Some conventions provide a minimum period of residence before the individual concerned is treated as "domiciled" in the State in which he is living. The aim of Article 4 is to avoid assessing the merits of national rules of law governing the circumstances in which a person is treated as domiciled in a Contracting State. However, Member countries, especially those whose domestic laws for determining a liability to tax are significantly different, may deal with this special case by including such a provision in their bilateral conventions.

II. COMMENTARY ON THE PROVISIONS OF THE ARTICLE

Paragraph 1

14. This paragraph provides a definition of the expression "person domiciled in a Contracting State" for the purposes of the Convention. The definition refers to the concept of domicile adopted in the domestic laws (see the Preliminary Remarks). As criteria for the taxation as a person domiciled in a Contracting State, the definition mentions domicile, residence, place of management or any other criterion of a similar nature.

15. As far as gift taxes are concerned, the Convention may also apply to persons other than individuals. The paragraph mentions in this respect the place of management as the criterion most generally used. In the case of charitable institutions, for which the criterion of "management" may often not apply, some similar criterion such as the "statutory seat" or the "establishment under the law of a certain State", may have to take its place.

16. Paragraph 1 also covers cases where an individual is deemed, under the taxation law of a State, to be domiciled in that State and on account of which his estate or gift is fully liable to tax therein although living in another State (for example, diplomats or other persons in government service). In accordance with the provisions of the second sentence of paragraph 1, however, a person is not to be considered a "person domiciled in a Contracting State" in the sense of the Convention if, although he is living in that State, his estate or gift is subject to tax only insofar as it includes property situated in that State. That situation exists in most States in relation to individuals, for example, foreign diplomatic and consular staff, serving in their territory.

Paragraph 2

17. In order to resolve the conflict arising because the deceased or the donor is considered by the domestic laws as being domiciled in both Contracting States at his death or at the time of the gift, it is necessary to establish special rules which give the attachment to one State a preference over the attachment to the other. As far as possible the "preference criterion" must be of such a nature that there can be no question but that

the person concerned will satisfy it in one State only, and at the same time it must reflect such an attachment that it is felt to be natural that the right to tax devolves upon that particular State.

18.   The Article gives preference to the Contracting State in which the deceased or the donor has a permanent home available to him. This criterion will frequently be sufficient to solve the conflict, for example, where an individual who has a permanent home in one Contracting State dies or makes a gift during a stay of some length in the other Contracting State.

19.   Subparagraph *a)* of paragraph 2 means, therefore, that in the application of the Convention (that is, where there is a conflict between the laws of the two States) it is considered that the domicile is that place where the individual owns or possesses a home; this home must be permanent, that is to say, the individual must have arranged and retained it for his permanent use as opposed to staying at a particular place under such conditions that it is evident that the stay is intended to be of short duration.

20.   As regards the concept of home, it should be observed that any form of home may be taken into account (house or apartment belonging to or rented by the individual, rented furnished room). However, the permanence of the home is essential; this means that the individual has arranged to have the dwelling available to him at all times continuously, and not occasionally for the purpose of a stay which, owing to the reasons for it, is necessarily of short duration (travel for pleasure, business travel, educational travel, attending a course at a school, etc.)

21.   If the deceased at his death, or the donor at the time of the gift, has a permanent home in both Contracting States, the Article gives preference to the State with which his personal and economic relations are closer, this being understood as the centre of vital interests. In the cases where the centre of vital interests cannot be determined, paragraph 2 provides as subsidiary criteria, firstly, habitual abode, and then nationality; if, when nationality is considered, the deceased or the donor is a national of both Contracting States or of neither of them, the question shall be solved by mutual agreement between the States concerned according to the procedure laid down in Article 11.

22.   Leaving aside what has just been said about short stays, subparagraph *a)* of paragraph 2 is applicable without it being necessary to have regard to any intention (unfulfilled) which the deceased or donor may have had to leave the home in order to settle elsewhere, or to any intention to return to a former domicile, for example, to his native country. In fact, the object of this subparagraph, in having regard solely to the actual home at the time of death or the gift, is precisely to avoid the necessity of determining directly what the individual wished or intended (intention of leaving or intention to return to a previous domicile). Determination of the individual's intention can give rise to endless disputes and, what is more, to manipulation on the part of the heirs.

23.   As already stated, subparagraph *a)* of paragraph 2 provides an additional criterion for the case where the deceased or donor has a permanent home in both Contracting States. In this case, the individual's domicile is considered to be in the Contracting State with which his personal and economic relations are closer (centre of vital interests).

24.   If the individual has a permanent home in both Contracting States, it is necessary to look at the facts in order to ascertain with which of the two States his personal and economic relations are closer. Thus, regard will be had to his family and social relations, his occupations, his political, cultural or other activities, his place of business, the place from which he administers his property, etc. The circumstances must be examined as a whole but it is nevertheless obvious that considerations based on the personal acts of the individual must receive special attention. If a person who has a home in one State sets up a second in the other State while retaining the first, the fact that he retains the first in the environment where he has always lived, where he has worked, and where he has his family and possessions, can, together with other elements, go to demonstrate that he has retained his centre of vital interests in the first State.

25.   Subparagraph *b)* of paragraph 2 establishes a secondary criterion for two quite distinct and different situations:

a)   the case where the individual has a permanent home available to him in both Contracting States and it is not possible to determine in which one he has his centre of vital interests;

b)   the case where the individual has a permanent home available to him in neither Contracting State.

Preference is given to the Contracting State where the individual has an habitual abode.

26.   In the first situation, the case where the individual has a permanent home available to him in both States, the fact of having an habitual abode in one State rather than in the other appears therefore as the circumstance which, in case of doubt as to where the individual has his centre of vital interests, tips the balance towards the State where he stays more frequently. For this purpose, regard must be had to stays made not only at the permanent home in the State in question but also at any other place in the same State.

27.   The second situation is the case of an individual who has a permanent home available to him in neither Contracting State, for example, a person going from one hotel to another. In this case also all stays made in a State must be considered without it being necessary to ascertain the reasons for them.

28.   In stipulating that, in the two situations which it contemplates, preference is given to the Contracting State where the individual has an habitual abode, subparagraph b) of paragraph 2 does not specify over what length of time the comparison must be made. The comparison must cover a sufficient length of time for it to be possible to determine whether the residence in each of the two States is habitual and to determine also the intervals at which the stays take place. It is difficult to fix such a time since, in the first situation and especially for estate and inheritance taxes, the comparison can be made only from the time when the deceased has an habitual abode in both States and, in the second situation, it can be made only from the time when the stays in each Contracting State commence. However, the date from which the comparison is possible may be very close to the date of death. Except insofar as the situations already mentioned have to be considered, the comparison must cover a sufficient length of time for it to be possible to determine whether the residence in each of the two States is habitual and to determine also the intervals at which the stays take place.

29.   Where, in the two situations referred to in subparagraph *b)*, the individual has an habitual abode in both Contracting States or in neither, subparagraph *c)* gives preference to the State of which he is a national. If the individual is a national of both Contracting States or of neither, subparagraph *d)* assigns to the competent authorities the duty of resolving the difficulty by mutal agreement according to the procedure established in Article 11.

Paragraph 3

30.   This paragraph concerns companies and other bodies of persons, irrespective of whether or not they are legal persons. It may be rare in practice for a company, etc. to be subject to tax on a domicile criterion in more than one State, but it is possible if, for example, one State attaches importance to the registration and the other State to the place of "management". So, in the case of companies or other bodies of persons, special rules as to the preference must also be established.

31.   It would not be an adequate solution to attach importance to a purely formal criterion like registration. Therefore paragraph 3 attaches importance to the place where the company, etc. is actually managed.

32.   As a result of these considerations, the "place of effective management" has been adopted as the preference criterion for persons other than individuals. The very rare cases where a charitable institution falls under paragraph 3 because it is, under paragraph 1, deemed to be domiciled in both Contracting States, may not always be solved by applying the criterion of "management", since that term refers more to business enterprises. In such a case the two Contracting States should rely on the mutual agreement procedure provided for in Article 11.

RESERVATIONS ON THE ARTICLE

33.   *Portugal* reserves the right to determine according to its domestic laws whether a person is domiciled in Portugal at the time of death or of making a gift.

34.   In accordance with the view expressed in connection with Article 1, *Turkey* and the *United States* reserve the right to impose tax on the total estate and gifts of their citizens, irrespective of the domicile at the time of death or gift.

COMMENTARY ON ARTICLE 5
CONCERNING TAXATION OF IMMOVABLE PROPERTY

Paragraph 1

1.   All double taxation conventions in force give the right to tax immovable property to the State in which such property is situated. Article 5 does not apply to immovable property situated in the Contracting State in which the deceased or the donor was domiciled within the meaning of Article 4 or situated in a third State; the provisions of Article 7 apply to such property.

2.   Paragraph 1 only applies to immovable property which forms part of the estate of, or of a gift made by, a person domiciled in a Contracting State. Property held by trustees is, under the law of some countries, not regarded as part of the trustees' estate while it may form part of the estate of the beneficiary or the settlor. In other circumstances, for example, where property is held by the trustees of a discretionary trust, the property usually will not form part of any person's estate. It is accepted that the State in which immovable property is situated should always have the right to tax such property and the definition provided in subparagraph a) of paragraph 1 of Article 3 will cover such cases. The same principle applies to property falling under Article 6.

Paragraph 2

3.   This paragraph defines immovable property by reference to the domestic law of the State of situs, This helps to avoid difficulties of interpretation as to whether an asset or a right is to be regarded as immovable property or not. The paragraph specifically mentions, however, the assets and rights which must always be regarded as immovable property. Such assets and rights are normally treated as immovable property under the laws or taxation rules of most Member countries. However, the paragraph provides that ships, boats and aircraft shall not be considered as immovable property.

4.   Article 5 extends also to any tangible movable property that had been placed on the immovable property so that it remained permanently attached thereto, and which thereby constitutes property acccessory, or annexed, to the immovable property within the meaning of the law of the State in which the immovable property is situated. Property accessory to immovable property follows the taxing rule for the immovable property even if temporarily separated from it.

5.   Furthermore, the expression "immovable property" includes, in particular, livestock and equipment of agricultural and forestry enterprises. According to paragraph 2, such livestock or equipment may be taxed in the State of *situs* of the immovable property in the exploitation of which the livestock or equipment is employed, even if at the time of death, or the gift, it was temporarily not on that property. No distinction is necessary according to whether or not, within the meaning of domestic law,

the livestock or equipment is intrinsically immovable or is regarded as immovable by its intended use. Nor is any distinction required according to whether or not the deceased or the donor was the owner of the immovable property in the exploitation of which the livestock or equipment he owned was employed by him.

6.   Debts secured on immovable property by mortgage or preferential right are to be treated as movable property. They are covered by the general rule in Article 7, unless, of course, Article 6 applies. Consequently if such debts form part of the business property employed in a permanent establishment of an enterprise, they may be taxed in the Contracting State in which the permanent establishment is situated. If, in view of the domestic laws of the Contracting States, it appears necessary to ensure against any difficulty of interpretation of the Convention on this point, paragraph 2 can be completed by adding the following words to the first sentence of the paragraph: "provided always that debts secured on immovable property by mortgage or otherwise shall not be regarded as immovable property".

Paragraph 3

7.   The general rule in paragraph 1 applies irrespective of the form of exploitation of the immovable property. Paragraph 3 makes it clear that this is the case in particular with immovable property of industrial, commercial and other enterprises and immovable property used for the performance of professional services or other activities of an independent character.

RESERVATION ON THE ARTICLE

8.   *Finland* reserves the right to tax shares or other corporate rights in Finnish companies, where the ownership of such shares or other corporate rights gives entitlement to the enjoyment of immovable property situated in Finland and owned or held by lease by the company.

COMMENTARY ON ARTICLE 6
CONCERNING TAXATION OF MOVABLE PROPERTY
OF A PERMANENT ESTABLISHMENT OR A FIXED BASE

Paragraph 1

1.   Following the practice established by many conventions already concluded, the Article gives the right to tax property (other than immovable property) forming part of the business property employed in the permanent establishment of an enterprise to the Contracting State in which the permanent establishment is situated. For property held by trustees, see paragraph 2 of the Commentary on Article 5.

2.   In the 1966 Estate Tax Draft, the taxation of ships and aircraft operated in international traffic, of boats engaged in inland waterways transport and of property, other than immovable property, pertaining to the operation of such ships, aircraft and boats was governed by a separate Article. This Article gave the right to tax such property to the State in which the place of effective management of the enterprise was situated and it was inserted mainly for the sake of conformity with the 1963 Income Tax Draft. The reason for such a special rule in an income tax convention lay in the difficulty of apportioning profits among the various permanent establishments of such an enterprise. Similar difficulties will not arise, however, in the scope of a convention of the present kind because it is easier to attribute the various assets to particular permanent establishments. In most cases the ships, aircraft and boats themselves will form part of the property of the head office. The attribution of property to a permanent establishment will therefore cover only the movable property such as office equipment. The Committee on Fiscal Affairs therefore decided to apply also to such ships, aircraft, boats and related property the provisions of Article 6 for death, inheritance and gift tax purposes. Member countries, however, are free to insert in their bilateral conventions a special provision relating to ships, aircraft and boats on the lines of the Article in the 1966 Estate Tax Draft.

3.   If the deceased or the donor was the owner of an enterprise with permanent establishments in various States, the State in which he was not domiciled is entitled to tax only the movable property employed in the permanent establishment situated in its territory. Any other movable property is taxable in the State of domicile in accordance with Article 7. Immovable property of an enterprise is not covered by Article 6. If such immovable property, regardless of the permanent establishment to which it is attributable, is situated in the Contracting State in which the deceased or donor is not domiciled, it may be taxed in that State (see paragraph 1 of the Commentary on Article 5); if situated elsewhere, Article 7 applies.

4.   Article 6 provides that the State in which the permanent establishment is situated may impose tax on movable property, wherever situated, forming part of the business property employed in the permanent establishment. This implies that, at the

time of death or the gift, the property was being used for the purposes of the enterprise and the relevant permanent establishment. The close connection between the property and the permanent establishment will usually be apparent from the accounts of the enterprise or from the tax returns made by the deceased or the donor before his death or before the gift. Debts, securities and other intangible property which are effectively connected with a permanent establishment or fixed base also come within this Article.

Paragraphs 2 to 5

5.   The definition of permanent establishment in paragraphs 2 to 5 is taken *verbatim* from paragraphs 1, 2, 3 and 4 of Article 5 of the 1977 Income Tax Model, so that only a brief explanation need be given here. Although more restricted in scope, these paragraphs apply in the same way to taxes on estates, inheritances and on gifts as they do to taxes on income. Consequently, the Commentary on the above-mentioned Article 5 applies equally to them, notwithstanding that it has not been reproduced here in its entirety.

Paragraph 2

6.   This paragraph gives a general definition of the concept of "permanent establishment" which brings out the essential characteristics of a permanent establishment, that is, a distinct *"situs"*, a "fixed place of business" through which the business of the enterprise is wholly or partly carried on, to the exclusion of any criterion based on its productive character or profitability.

Paragraph 3

7.   This paragraph contains a list, by no means exhaustive, of examples, each of which can be regarded, *prima facie,* as constituting a permanent establishment. As these examples are to be seen against the background of the general definition given in paragraph 2, it is assumed that the Contracting States interpret the terms listed, "a place of management", "a branch", "an office", etc., in such a way that such places of business constitute permanent establishments only if they meet the requirements of paragraph 2.

Paragraph 4

8.   This paragraph expressly provides that a building site or construction or installation project constitutes a permanent establishment only if it lasts more than twelve months. Any of the items listed which does not meet this condition does not of itself constitute a permanent establishment, even if there is within it an installation, for example, an office or a workshop within the meaning of paragraph 3, associated with the construction activity. The provision that a building site or assembly project shall only be deemed to be a permanent establishment if it exists for more than twelve months is not intended to prevent a country from imposing estate, inheritance or gift tax where a year has not expired at the time of death or the gift if it appears that the site or project is likely to last for more than twelve months.

Paragraph 5

9.   This paragraph lists a number of business activities which are treated as exceptions to the general definition laid down in paragraph 2 and which are not

permanent establishments even if the activity is carried on through a fixed place of business. The common feature of these activities is that they are, in general, preparatory or auxiliary activities. This is laid down explicitly in the case of the exception mentioned in subparagraph *e)* which actually amounts to a general restriction of the scope of the definition contained in paragraph 2. Moreover, subparagraph *f)* provides that combinations of activities mentioned in subparagraphs *a)* to *e)* in the same fixed place of business shall be deemed not to be a permanent establishment, provided that the overall activity of the fixed place of business resulting from this combination is of a preparatory or auxiliary character. Thus the provisions of paragraph 5 are designed to prevent an enterprise of one State from being taxed in the other State, if it carries on in that other State, activities of a purely preparatory or auxiliary character. There may be reasons for restricting these exceptions in a convention on taxes on the transfer of capital on the occasion of death or a gift, since they may, although not being profit-producing, involve the existence of capital assets in the country concerned. The Committee on Fiscal Affairs decided, however, that it would be better if the exceptions were kept in line with those mentioned in paragraph 4 of Article 5 of the 1977 Income Tax Model.

10.   Subparagraph *a)* relates only to the case in which an enterprise acquires the use of facilities for storing, displaying or delivering its own goods or merchandise. Subparagraph *b)* relates to the stock of merchandise itself and provides that the stock as such shall not be treated as a permanent establishment if it is maintained for the purpose of storage, display or delivery. Subparagraph *c)* covers the case in which a stock of goods or merchandise belonging to one enterprise is processed by a second enterprise on behalf of, or for the account of, the first-mentioned enterprise. Subparagraph *d)* relates to fixed places of business used solely for purchasing goods or merchandise or for collecting information. This wording is intended to include the case of the newspaper bureau which has no purpose other than to act as one of many "tentacles" of the parent body; to exempt such a bureau is no more than an extension of the concept of "mere purchase".

11.   Subparagraph *e)* provides that a fixed place of business is not deemed to be a permanent establishment if the only activities of the enterprise carried out there are of a preparatory or auxiliary character. The wording of this subparagraph makes it unnecessary to produce an exhaustive list of exceptions. Furthermore, this subparagraph provides a generalised exception to the definition in paragraph 2 and, when read with that paragraph, provides a more selective test by which to determine what constitutes a permanent establishment. To a considerable degree it limits that definition and excludes from its rather wide scope a number of forms of business organisations which, although they are carried on through a fixed place of business, should not be treated as permanent establishments (see also paragraphs 23 to 28 of the Commentary on Article 5 of the 1977 Income Tax Model).

12.   A fixed place of business used both for activities which rank as an exception (paragraph 5) and for other activities would be regarded as a single permanent establishment and property relating to both types of activites would be taxable. This would be the case, for example, where a store maintained for the delivery of goods is also engaged in sales.

13.   The provisions of paragraphs 5 and 6 of Article 5 of the 1977 Income Tax Model, dealing with dependent and independent agents, and of paragraph 7 of Article 5 of the same Model, dealing with associated companies, have not been taken over in this Convention since it is the aim here to lay down principles for allocating the right to tax transfers of capital on the occasion of death or a gift. These provisions will not normally

be relevant in that context. However, if Member countries consider these provisions are relevant, they are free to include them in their bilateral conventions.

Paragraph 6

14.   The term "fixed base" is not defined in the Article. It would cover, for example, a physician's consulting room or the office of an architect or a lawyer. A person performing professional services would probably not as a rule have premises of this kind in any State other than that of his domicile. However, if there is in another State a centre of activity of a fixed or permanent character, then that State should be entitled to tax the property employed in that centre.

15.   The term "professional services" includes, especially, independent scientific, literary, artistic, educational or teaching activities, a well as the independent activities of physicians, lawyers, engineers, architects, dentists and accountants, excluding professional services performed in employment, for example, a physician serving as a medical officer in a factory. The above enumeration simply gives a few typical examples by way of explanation and is not exhaustive. Apart from the professions just listed, paragraph 6 also applies to all other independent activities of a similar character. Difficulties of interpretation which might arise in special cases may be solved by mutual agreement between the competent authorities of the Contracting States.

OBSERVATION ON THE COMMENTARY

16.   *Italy* does not adhere to the interpretation given in paragraph 7 above concerning the list of examples. In its opinion, these examples can always be regarded as constituting *a priori* permanent establishments.

RESERVATIONS ON THE ARTICLE

Shipping

17.   In view of its particular situation in relation to shipping, *Greece* wishes to retain its freedom of action regarding the taxation of ships and boats of every description.

18.   The *United Kingdom* reserves the right to include a separate Article covering enterprises operating ships, boats and aircraft so that such property may be taxed in the State in which the enterprise is effectively managed.

19.   The *United States* reserves the right to include a separate Article covering enterprises operating ships, boats, aircraft and container leasing operations, so that such property may be taxed in the State in which the individual operating such enterprise is domiciled.

Paragraph 1

20.   In view of the special aspects of their domestic laws referred to in their reservations on Article 1, *Belgium* and *Luxembourg* reserve the right to tax property falling under Article 6 in all cases where such property is the subject of a gift certified by a title governed and protected by their laws.

21.   Referring to their reservations on Article 7 as regards certain items of movable property, *France, Greece, Italy, New Zealand, Portugal, Turkey,* the *United Kingdom* and the *United States* reserve the right to adapt paragraph 1 of Article 6 so as to enable those States to tax similar items of movable property forming part of the business property of a permanent establishment which an enterprise has in the other Contracting State.

Paragraph 4

22.   *Greece, Portugal* and *Turkey* reserve the right to consider that any building site or construction or installation project which lasts more than six months should be regarded as a permanent establishment.

23.   *Spain* reserves its position on paragraph 4 so as to be able to tax an enterprise having a permanent establishment in Spain, even if the site of the construction or installation project does not last for more than twelve months, where the activity of this enterprise in Spain presents a certain degree of permanency within the meaning of paragraphs 2 and 3.

COMMENTARY ON ARTICLE 7
CONCERNING TAXATION OF OTHER PROPERTY

I.   PRELIMINARY REMARKS

1.   The rules concerning liability to taxes on estates and inheritances and on gifts vary greatly from country to country. Various criteria may be adopted to determine whether taxes become due on the occasion of death or of a gift and what is the taxable property. The causes of double taxation with regard to taxes on estates and inheritances and on gifts are thus numerous.

2.   In most Member countries the domestic law imposes tax on the total assets of the estate or gift wherever the property is situated (that is, comprehensive tax liability) but does so by reference to criteria which vary from country to country. Some of those criteria are mentioned in paragraphs 5 and 6 of the Commentary on Article 1, for example, domicile, residence, nationality of the deceased or the donor. Some States also impose a comprehensive tax liability on the parts of an estate or a gift which are transferred to an heir, legatee or donee who is domiciled or resident in, or a national of, such a State. In certain States a comprehensive tax liability may, in the case of trusts, be based on the domicile of the settlor or by reference to the State under whose law the trust was established. On the other hand most States also tax transfers of all or certain property situated within their territory, even if the criteria mentioned above are not satisfied (limited tax liability).

3.   The aim of the Convention is to eliminate the double taxation that can arise from the operation of various domestic laws on the occasion of the death or gift. The Convention seeks to achieve this aim principally by limiting the right to tax to two States which are the State of *situs* of the property within the meaning of Articles 5 and 6 and the State in which the deceased or donor is domiciled within the meaning of Article 4, thus excluding any other criteria which may be used under domestic law as bases for comprehensive tax liability. Any double taxation remaining between the State of *situs* and the State of domicile will be eliminated by applying the provisions of Articles 9A or 9B.

II.   TAXATION BY THE STATE OF THE DECEASED'S
OR THE DONOR'S DOMICILE

4.   Article 7 gives to the State of the deceased's or the donor's domicile the sole taxation right in respect of the transfer of any kind of property which is not dealt with in Articles 5 and 6. That right extends not only to property of a class not expressly

mentioned in those Articles but also to any immovable property situated in the State of domicile or in a third State, and to any movable property which is not attributable to a permanent establishment or a fixed base which is situated in the other Contracting State.

III. TAXATION BY THE STATE OF THE DECEASED'S OR THE DONOR'S NATIONALITY

5.   Where one Contracting State imposes tax because the deceased or the donor possesses its nationality and the other Contracting State imposes tax because the deceased or the donor is domiciled there, Article 7 gives priority to the right to tax of the State of domicile and, subject to any provision to the contrary, implies that the first State relinquishes its right to tax. This is justified because that right to tax should belong, at least in the first instance, to the State with which the deceased's or the donor's personal and economic relations are closer, which is normally the State of domicile rather than the State of nationality, and further by the fact that only a few Member countries tax according to nationality. It may be added that the balance would not be equal if provision had to be made for credit against the tax due to the State of domicile for part of the tax due to the State of nationality; from the point of view of those States whose law does not impose tax according to nationality, giving such a credit would amount to the unilateral relinquishment of their right to tax on the basis of domicile without receiving any *quid pro quo.*

6.   However, taxation by the State of nationality does not lead to double taxation once it is only subsidiary to taxation by the State of domicile. In other words, double taxation is avoided once the States which impose estate, inheritance or gift tax according to nationality allow a credit, not only for the tax imposed in other States on the basis of situs, but also for the tax levied by the State of domicile. The State of nationality, of course, is not required to give a credit for tax imposed by the State of domicile on property which the State of nationality can tax under the provisions of Articles 5 and 6. This procedure should give satisfaction to States which view the taxation by the State of nationality as a safeguard against their nationals leaving the country for another where the tax is lower. Elimination of double taxation and prevention of tax avoidance are thus achieved simultaneously: there is no longer any advantage in leaving the State of nationality if, in aggregate, at least as much tax has to be paid as would have been levied by that State; double taxation is avoided by the credit method. The need for preventing tax avoidance by such means only arises, however, if the death or the gift occurs within a limited period after the person transferred his domicile from his State of nationality to another State; for this purpose, a time limit of ten years would seem ample. The Contracting States are free in their bilateral agreements to adapt the Convention in this sense. A model provision is given in the Commentary on Articles 9A and 9B (see paragraphs 72 *et seq.*). The ten-year period mentioned in this model provision is a maximum period and the Contracting States are free to agree upon a shorter one.

7.   The model provision given in paragraph 73 of the Commentary on Articles 9A and 9B can, if necessary, be expanded to cover the case where a person, who was not a national of one Contracting State, has moved to the other Contracting State within a short time before death or making a gift. This is a matter for bilateral negotiation.

IV. TAXATION BY THE STATE OF THE HEIR'S OR THE DONEE'S DOMICILE, OR BY ANY OTHER CRITERION FOR COMPREHENSIVE TAX LIABILITY

8.   In the case of the death of, or of a gift made by, a person domiciled in one of the Contracting States, the allocation of the right to tax by the Convention precludes any imposition of estate or gift tax by the other State by reason of the domicile of the heirs, legatees or donees, or by any other criterion leading to a comprehensive tax liability (see, however, paragraphs 72 *et seq.* of the Commentary on Articles 9A and 9B).

V. TAXATION BY THE STATE OF *SITUS*

9.   As regards the conflict between the State of *situs* and the State of the deceased's or the donor's domicile, the Convention gives to the State of *situs* the right to tax immovable property (Article 5), movable property forming part of the business property of a permanent establishment of an enterprise (Article 6), and movable property pertaining to a fixed base used for the performance of professional services or other activities of an independent character (Article 6). In respect of all other property the right to tax is given to the State of domicile (Article 7).

10.   According to the Convention, tangible movable property considered as property accessory to immovable property, such as livestock and equipment employed in agricultural and forestry enterprises, may be taxed in the State where it is situated (Article 5); tangible movable property forming part of the business property of a permanent establishment of an enterprise, or pertaining to a fixed base used for the performance of professional services or other activities of an independent character, may be taxed in the State in which the permanent establishment or the fixed base is situated (Article 6). All other tangible movable property, such as furniture, linen, household goods, collections of pictures or other objets d'art, jewellery, pleasure craft and bank notes, is taxable only in the State of the deceased's or the donor's domicile. In view of the minimal balance of advantage to Member countries as a whole and to persons' estates or gifts in general, practical considerations certainly support this solution. However, States remain free to stipulate in bilateral conventions that tangible movable property not covered by Articles 5 and 6, or certain categories of such property, may be taxed in the State in which it was situated at the time of the death or the gift. Such taxation rights should, however, be limited to very special cases and, to avoid any dispute, it would be desirable if the convention contained a list of the categories of tangible movable property which the country of *situs* may tax. Due care should be taken to ensure that, in the case of Contracting States which use the exemption method (Article 9A) for the avoidance of double taxation, no abuse of the convention may be made possible by such a special rule, especially for property which can easily be moved from one country to another.

VI. TAXATION OF DEBTS, SECURITIES AND SIMILAR RIGHTS

11.   The principle adopted in Article 7 is a compromise between the positions of the various States. The attribution to the State of *situs* of the right to tax not only immovable property, but also the other types of property designated in Article 6, constitutes a

considerable concession for a number of States. It has not been considered possible to go further and attribute also the right to tax debts, securities in general and similar rights (company shares and debentures, government securities, etc.) to the State where these are deemed to be situated (domicile of the debtor, registered office of the company which issued the shares, place of deposit of bearer securities, etc.). Such an extension would involve sacrifices only by the States – the most numerous moreover – which limit the basis of tax on the death of, or the making of a gift by, a person domiciled abroad, to immovable property and particular categories of movable property having a physical situation in the territory of the State or which are of a permanent character tending to assimilate them to immovable property. Similarly the balance of concessions would not be equal if different treatment were accorded to registered shares and bearer shares, owing to the differences in the laws of the various States as to the form in which the shareholder's title is evidenced. While in certain States registration is the rule, in most Member countries the bearer share has become very general. It is not possible for the latter countries to discriminate, in the rules for taxing shares in their companies, between registered and bearer shares as there is no intrinsic difference between them; only the forms, which moreover are often interchangeable, are different.

12.   Apart from the considerations in paragraph 11, the division of the right to tax according to Articles 5 to 7 is further justified on practical grounds. Usually it is the State of domicile that is best, and sometimes the only one, equiped to check the declaration for tax purposes of securities left by the deceased or given by the donor. This is certainly true in the case of bearer securities, this being the form in which, in the States of Continental Europe, government bonds or shares and debentures of companies or other institutions are generally evidenced. As regards registered shares in companies incorporated in States where the registered form alone is possible, it should be observed that shares owned by foreigners are very often registered not in the name of the beneficial owner but in the name of nominees against whom the beneficial owner can enforce his right, so that the death of, or the making of a gift by, the beneficial owner remains unknown in the State in which the company is incorporated.

13.   In attributing the right to tax, it is also desirable to avoid a system which would allow the taxpayer the possibility of himself determining by his financial arrangements in which State the tax is payable. For example, a person who is domiciled in State A makes over (in return for shares) debts and securities situated or deemed to be situated in State B to a holding company established in State A, practically all the shares in which are owned by him. If the principle that shares are taxable in the State where the company is established were adopted, it would follow that when that person died the right to tax belonged to State A. State B would levy no tax because the securities situated in State B would not have devolved on his death. Conversely, it would be possible to create a source of liability to tax in State B by conveying to a holding company established in State B debts and securities situated in State A. The attribution of the right to tax such movable property only to the State of domicile makes the taxation independent of such arrangements.

14.   The division of the right to tax according to Articles 5 to 7 is also more practical from the point of view of the taxpayer. The heirs of a person who has left immovable property or a permanent establishment of an enterprise in a State not that of his domicile have of course to carry out various formalities in that State, the declaration of the estate for tax purposes being one amongst others. It is, however, quite another matter if the deceased leaves securities originating in a State with which he may be entirely

unconnected. The deceased may even leave securities originating in several States. Dispersal of liability to tax amongst these States, with the declaration formalities and resulting expense, is certainly not to be recommended.

VII. TAXATION OF INTERESTS IN ASSOCIATIONS OF INDIVIDUALS AND OTHER CONFLICTS OF TREATMENT

15.   Sometimes the Contracting States may not agree as to whether a particular asset falls under Articles 5 and 6 or under Article 7. If there is disagreement as to whether a certain asset is immovable or movable property, the question is settled by paragraph 2 of Article 5. If there is disagreement as to whether or not a movable asset is to be attributed to a permanent establishment or a fixed base, such questions of fact have to be solved by the mutual agreement procedure.

16.   There are, however, other situations where the disagreement may be based not on a question of fact, but on a question of law. A number of such situations are described in the following paragraphs and a way of solving these disagreements is suggested in paragraph 24.

A.   Interests in a partnership

17.   The rules in Articles 5 and 6 apply to the types of property enumerated in those Articles, irrespective of whether the deceased or the donor was the sole owner of the property or owned it in common with others by inheritance, acquisition in common or otherwise. In a certain number of Member countries, civil associations and commercial associations of individuals in which the members have unlimited liability do not constitute legal persons distinct from their members; thus, notwithstanding the existence of the instrument of association, the property held in common is considered to belong directly to the members so that, on the death of, or the making of a gift by, a member, his share is taxable in exactly the same way as property of which he is the sole owner; in this case the application of the rules in Articles 5 and 6 presents no difficulty.

18.   Although under the domestic laws of some Member countries a partnership is not treated as a legal person distinct from its members, property held in common may not be treated as belonging directly to the members. Where this is the case the consequences are the same as in paragraph 20 below.

19.   In other countries, civil associations and commercial associations of individuals in which the members have unlimited liability are regarded as distinct legal persons. Unless any special provisions exist to the contrary, it is necessary, on the death of, or the making of a gift by, a member of such an association, to have regard, not directly to a share of the association's property and debts, but to intangible movable property in the nature of a right, that is, a capital interest in the association, constituting a distinct item of property. In certain Member countries such interests are liable to estate, inheritance or gift tax even if the deceased or donor is domiciled abroad.

20.   The problems outlined in the previous paragraphs may lead to a conflict of treatment as far as the taxation rules of Articles 5 and 6 on the one hand, and Article 7 on the other hand, are concerned.

68

EXAMPLE 1

The deceased was domiciled in State A. He left an interest in a partnership established in State B. The whole property of the partnership is movable property of a permanent establishment situated in State B. The laws of the Contracting States differ as to the treatment of such an interest.

First case: State A regards such an interest as a kind of co-ownership whereas State B regards it as an interest in money's worth (like shares in a company). If State A is a country using the exemption method under Article 9A it would refrain from taxing the interest since, under its domestic law, the interest is considered to be property belonging to a permanent establishment situated in State B. State B would also refrain from taxing the interest since, under its domestic law, the deceased left only property falling under Article 7. Double non-taxation would therefore arise.

Second case: State A regards such an interest as an interest in money's worth (like shares in a company) whereas State B regards it as a kind of co-ownership. State A would tax the property and would not give any relief under Articles 9A or 9B. State B would consider the property to belong to a permanent establishment situated in its territory and would tax it under Article 6. Unrelieved double taxation would therefore arise.

B. Undistributed estates

21. A similar conflict can arise in cases of undistributed estates and is illustrated by the following example.

EXAMPLE 2

A person, X, dies domiciled in State A and leaves immovable property situated in State B to his heir, Y. Y dies before the estate has been fully administered, leaving his property to his heir, Z. Both Y and Z are also domiciled in State A.

Under the laws of most Member countries the transfer of property from heir Y to heir Z would be a transfer of immovable property which Y inherited from X. Those countries will apply the rules of Article 5 to that property. However, due regard is to be had to the fact that, in some States, until the estate of X has been fully administered, no actual ownership has been transferred from X to Y. Therefore, the domestic laws of some States take the view that Z did not inherit immovable property from Y but only the right of Y to have that immovable property transferred to him. Such States treat this right of Y as an incorporal right and consequently as property falling under Article 7. By such divergencies of law, conflicts similar to those described in paragraph 20 above may occur.

C. Property held in trust

22. Where property falling under Articles 5 or 6 is held in trust, conflicts similar to those described in paragraphs 15 to 21 above may occur if one State regards the beneficiary's interest as an interest in the trust, and so falling under Article 7, and the other State regards the beneficiary's interest as an interest in the property held in the trust, and so falling under Articles 5 or 6.

D.   Companies holding immovable property

23.   Furthermore, some States regard the transfer on death, or the making of a gift, of all or a part of the shares in a company whose only or principal assets are immovable property as a transfer of all or part of the immovable property of the company. Since not all States share this view similar conflicts as described above may arise.

E.   Possible solutions

24.   States that wish to avoid these and other conflicts of treatment could insert in their bilateral conventions a provision along the following lines:

> "If by the law of a Contracting State any right or interest is regarded as property not falling under Article 5 or 6, but by the law of the other Contracting State that right or interest is regarded as property falling under either of those Articles, then the nature of the right or interest shall be determined by the law of the State which is not the State of the deceased's or the donor's domicile".

25.   The effect of such a provision can be illustrated by the following example:

EXAMPLE 3

The deceased died domiciled in State A. He left to his heir a 50% interest in a partnership established in State B. The assets of the partnership consist of the following property:

a)	Immovable property situated	
	In State A	100
	In State B	100
	In a third State	100
b)	Movable property attributable to permanent establishments	
	In State A	300
	In State B	300
	In a third State	300
		1,200

The value of the interest in the partnership amounts therefore to 600.

First case: State A regards that interest as an interest in a company whereas State B regards it as a kind of co-ownership.

Under the Convention (without the provision in paragraph 24) State A would tax the full amount of the interest (600) as falling under Article 7. State B would tax, under Articles 5 and 6, 50% of the immovable property situated in its territory and 50% of the movable property which is attributable to the permanent establishment situated in its territory. State A would neither exempt nor give credit for the tax on the property taxed in State B. Unrelieved double taxation would therefore arise.

By inserting the proposed provision, State B would keep the right to tax the same property (50 + 150) as before, but State A would have to either exempt, or give credit for State B's tax on, that property. The right of State A to tax the interest, as far as property situated in a third State is concerned, comes from the application of Article 7.

Second case: State A regards the interest as a kind of co-ownership whereas State B regards it as an interest in a company.

Under the Convention (without the provision in paragraph 24) State B would lose its right to tax since it regards the interest as falling under Article 7. If State A is a country using the exemption method, it would lose its right to tax the share of the immovable property and of the permanent establishment situated in State B. Double non-taxation would therefore arise.

By inserting the proposed provision State A would retain its right to tax.

26.   Notwithstanding the solution proposed in paragraph 24, it may be reasonable for the State in which the deceased or donor was not domiciled to retain a right to tax the partnership interest to the extent that the partnership owns immovable property or has a permanent establishment in that State. If necessary a specific provision should be added in bilateral negotiations to provide for this right.

27.   If Member countries consider that the solution proposed in paragraph 24 does not resolve all conflicts of treatment satisfactorily, they are free to adopt an alternative solution. For example, in the case of partnerships, they may resolve this problem in bilateral negotiations by determining the nature of the property by reference to the law of the State under which the partnership is established.

VIII.   SPECIAL FEATURES OF THE DOMESTIC LAWS OF CERTAIN MEMBER COUNTRIES

28.   The special taxation rules imposed by some Member countries may make it necessary to adapt Article 7 to deal with property held by trustees. Ordinarily the right to impose tax under Article 7 depends upon the domicile of the person to whom the transfer is imputed. In the case of trust property, if Article 7 is not clarified, there may be uncertainty as to whom the transfer is imputed and, as a result, a State may find that Article 7 has the unintended effect of depriving it of a charge over property held in trust which it should retain. In some circumstances, for example, where the other State imposes no tax, this could result in double non-taxation of the trust property. The same applies to all other similar situations outlined in paragraph 26 of the Commentary on Article 1.

29.   As previously explained (see paragraph 2 of the Commentary on Article 5), trust property is not usually part of a beneficiary's estate although it may be so treated for tax purposes in some States. The inclusion in Article 3 of the definition of the term "property which forms part of the estate, etc ..." should, in general, ensure that Article 7 will not require modification where taxes are imposed on an "interest in possession" trust and both States impute the transfer to the intervening beneficiary. In other cases, as

indicated in paragraph 26 of the Commentary on Article 1, it may be necessary to ensure that the Convention applies to the special taxation imposed on property held in trust. When in such other cases Article 1 is modified to take account of the special taxation rules imposed by a Member country and to identify an imputed transferor other than the intervening beneficiary, a parallel modification should be made to Article 7 to make it clear that the Convention applies to give to the State of the imputed transferor's domicile the exclusive right to tax all property subject to an imputed transfer, other than property falling under Articles 5 or 6.

IX. AVOIDANCE OF FACTUAL NON-TAXATION

30.   To some extent Article 7 limits the right of the State which is not the State of domicile to exercise its domestic tax law. Where that State, under its domestic law, imposes merely a limited tax liability, the loss of tax revenue will relate only to certain categories of movable property situated in its territory. Where that State imposes however, under its domestic law, a comprehensive tax liability (for example, by reason of the nationality of the deceased or the domicile or the nationality of the heir) the loss of tax revenue will also relate to any property situated in the other Contracting State or in a third State.

31.   Some States, when giving up a taxation right in favour of another State under the Convention, may sometimes want to have the assurance that the tax which should then be levied in the other State can be collected there. The difficulties in the collection may be illustrated by the following example:

EXAMPLE 4

The deceased was domiciled in State A. He left to his heir, domiciled in State B, bank accounts:

a) in State A		100
b) in State B		10,000
c) in a third State		10,000

Under Article 7, State A has the sole right to tax all three bank accounts. State B, although it may, under its domestic law, also have a full taxation right by reason of the domicile of the heir, may no longer tax that estate. However, since the only asset of the estate available in State A is a bank account of 100, State A may not be able to enforce its tax claim.

32.   The simplest way of avoiding such a situation would be to conclude a convention for mutual assistance in the collection of taxes in general. Member countries which do not want, or are unable to go that far, but which want to avoid such situations, are free to adopt in their bilateral conventions on estates, inheritances and gifts a separate Article providing for such assistance for the taxes covered by the convention.

33.   Some States, which for some reason could not conclude between themselves such a mutual assistance convention or Article, have adopted in their conventions another solution. This solution involves the addition to Article 7 of a second paragraph which provides that the State in which the deceased or donor was not domiciled may impose its domestic tax to the extent that tax has not been paid in the State of domicile. This

provision applies notwithstanding the provisions of paragraph 1 of Article 7, but does not apply where no tax was paid in the State of domicile as a result of a specific exemption, deduction, credit or allowance there. Member countries wishing to include such a provision are free to do so in their bilateral negotiations.

OBSERVATION ON THE COMMENTARY

34. *Switzerland* considers that rights to tax conceded on the basis of criteria mentioned in Chapters III to V of the Commentary are only subsidiary ones, which could not restrict the primary right to tax established by Article 7 (the donor's domicile or the deceased's last domicile). The State to which this subsidiary right to tax is conceded must take account of the primary right to tax of the other State by granting credit for that State's tax against its own tax. Solutions suggested in paragraphs 70 *et seq.* of the Commentary on Article 9 might be followed, as the case may be, for this purpose.

RESERVATIONS ON THE ARTICLE

35. *Austria* reserves the right to impose a subsidiary comprehensive tax liability by reason of the domicile of the heir, legatee, donee or other beneficiary, whenever the other Contracting State makes use, in bilateral negotiations, of any of its reservations concerning the basic principles of the Model.

36. In view of the special aspects of their domestic laws referred to in their reservations on Article 1, *Belgium* and *Luxembourg* reserve the right to tax property falling under Article 7 in all cases where such property is the subject of a gift certified by a title governed and protected by their laws.

37. *Finland* makes a reference to its reservation on Article 5.

38. *France, Portugal* and *Spain* cannot accept this Article without reservations. When negotiating bilateral conventions, these countries wish to reserve the right to exclude from the scope of this Article certain items of property, in particular securities, which are deemed to be situated in their territories under domestic laws.

39. *Germany* reserves the right to impose a subsidiary comprehensive tax liability by reason of the domicile of the heir, legatee, donee or other beneficiary.

40. In view of its particular situation in relation to shipping, *Greece* wishes to retain its freedom of action regarding the taxation of ships and boats of every description. Greece reserves its position and wishes to maintain its right to tax some items which are considered to be situated in Greece according to the Greek legislation, such as shares of Greek companies and debts secured on immovable property situated in Greece or on ships registered under the Greek flag. Moreover, Greece reserves the right to impose taxes on the property of Greek nationals according to its internal legislation.

41. In view of the fact that its domestic laws adopt the criterion of *situs* as the criterion of taxation, *Italy* wishes, in negotiating bilateral agreements, to preserve its right to tax debts and securities which are situated, or deemed to be situated, in its territory.

42.   *New Zealand* reserves its position on this Article, and would wish to maintain its right to tax shares in companies incorporated in New Zealand or registered in a branch register in New Zealand.

43.   According to Turkish fiscal legislation all property situated in Turkish territory, even that belonging to non-Turkish nationals, is liable to taxes on estates, inheritances and gifts. *Turkey* therefore reserves the right to tax movable property which is situated or deemed to be situated in its territory.

44.   The *United Kingdom* is unable to accept this Article so far as it applies to company shares. In negotiating bilateral agreements the United Kingdom wishes to reserve the right to tax registered shares in companies incorporated in its territory.

45.   The *United States* reserves the right, in negotiating bilateral treaties, to impose tax on intangible personal property which under its laws has a *situs* in the United States.

COMMENTARY ON ARTICLE 8
CONCERNING THE DEDUCTION OF DEBTS

I. PRELIMINARY REMARKS

1. Article 8, dealing with the deduction of debts, is normally not important as far as gift taxes are concerned, but it is of major importance for estate and inheritance taxes. The following paragraphs, therefore, mainly refer to death duties. Where necessary they should be applied to gift taxes.

2. There are considerable differences in the way in which the domestic laws of Member countries deal with debts, particularly where the deceased person dies domiciled abroad. For example, certain States allow no debts as a deduction; others allow the deduction of a proportionate fraction of the total debts of the estate, some allow the deduction of debts connected, economically or otherwise, with the property which is taxable according to their law; finally, others allow the deduction of all debts contracted or payable within that State.

3. A convention for the avoidance of double taxation has, in the first instance, to divide the taxation rights over the assets of the estate between the Contracting States. This division should logically be accompanied by a division of the obligation to deduct the debts of the estate. The failure to provide for a proper division of debts between the Contracting States may lead to double taxation or to double non-taxation or to an inequitable taxation treatment of a deceased person's estate.

4. The difficulty of finding a solution which is satisfactory from all points of view no doubt explains why the conventions concluded between Member countries contain different rules for the allocation of debts. Certain conventions adopt the proportional method. Others adopt a method based on the connection there may be between the debts and particular property. The 1966 Estate Tax Draft adopted the latter method.

5. The Fiscal Committee took that decision in 1966 because the majority of Member countries had shown a preference for this method as it accorded best with their domestic laws. There is no reason to deviate from that decision in this Model. The text presented does not, however, prevent a State which is concluding a convention with another State whose domestic law divides debts proportionally to the amount of the estate, from adopting that method by bilateral agreement. Nor *a fortiori* does it prevent States whose domestic laws are based on the proportional method from adopting it in the conventions concluded between themselves.

6. Article 8 is not intended to cover pecuniary legacies (see paragraph 48 *et seq* below).

II. COMMENTARY ON THE PROVISIONS OF THE ARTICLE

A. Allocation of debts

Paragraphs 1 to 3

7.   These paragraphs provide general rules for the allocation of debts according to economic links. The rules are as follows:

a) *Debts falling under paragraphs 1 and 2*

8.   Paragraphs 1 and 2 deal with debts which are secured on, or in the way specified in the paragraphs are economically connected with, property which may, under the provisions of Articles 5 and 6, be taxed in the State which is not the State of domicile of the deceased person. Such debts are required to be deducted from the value of the property on which they are secured or with which they are economically connected.

b) *Debts falling under paragraph 3*

9.   Paragraph 3 deals with all other kinds of debts, for example:

- debts secured on, or economically connected with, movable property falling under Article 7;
- debts secured on, or economically connected with, immovable property situated either in the State of the deceased's domicile or in a third State;
- debts which are neither secured on, nor have any economic connection with, any asset of the estate (hospital bills, funeral expenses, etc.).

Such debts have to be deducted from the property which, under the provisions of Article 7, is taxable only in the State of the deceased's domicile.

c) *Implication of paragraphs 1 to 3 for the State of situs*

10.   These rules imply for the State which is not the State of domicile of the deceased person:

- i) that this State deducts the debts falling under paragraphs 1 and 2 from the value of the property which it taxes according to Articles 5 and 6, even if, under its domestic law, it would not allow the deduction of any debts when taxing as a *situs* country; and
- ii) that this State, subject to paragraph 5, refrains from deducting any other debts (that is debts falling under paragraph 3), even if its domestic law would permit such a deduction.

11.   Member countries must accept the first obligation unless they have entered a reservation against this Article. Member countries which cannot accept the second consequence should stress that point in bilateral negotiations (see on this point, however, paragraphs 32 *et seq.* below).

d) *Implication of paragraphs 1 to 3 for the State of domicile*

12.   The rules explained in paragraphs 8 and 9 above impose on the State of domicile the obligation of deducting the debts falling under paragraphs 1 and 2 of the Article from the property which may be taxed in the other State. The net value so ascertained is the value on which relief is to be given under Articles 9A (Exemption Method) or 9B (Credit Method). The State of domicile has to deduct the debts falling under paragraph 3 of the Article from that part of the estate which is taxable only in that

State. The net value so ascertained is not subject to any relief under Articles 9A or 9B.

13.   States which apply the exemption method have to exempt from their tax, subject to progressivity, the net value of the property which may be taxed in the other Contracting State. Such States do not then deduct any debts covered by paragraphs 1 and 2 from the value of other property. They do not deduct such debts even if they exceed the value of the property falling under Articles 5 and 6 (see, however, paragraphs 22 *et seq.* below).

14.   The allocation of debts explained in the foregoing paragraph has to be made in the State of domicile even if the property falling under Articles 5 and 6 has not actually been taxed in the other State.

15.   States which apply the credit method have to allow from their own tax a deduction for the tax levied in the other State on the property which may be taxed in that other State, up to the amount of their own tax attributable to the net value (computed as in paragraph 12 above) of such property.

16.   Most Member countries have embodied within their domestic laxs unilateral rules for the allocation of debts. Should such rules produce more favourable results for the taxpayer than the rules of the Convention, some States may have to apply their domestic law (the consequences of this are set out in paragraphs 37 *et seq.* below).

17.   The implementation of paragraphs 1 to 3 may be illustrated by the following examples:

EXAMPLE 1 (to paragraphs 1 and 2)

The deceased died domiciled in State A. His estate consists of:

Movable property	200
Immovable property situated in State B	100
Gross estate	300
A debt economically connected with the immovable property (see paragraph 1)	–60
Net estate	240

State B, under its domestic law, does not deduct any debts.

Taxation under domestic law:

	State A	State B
Movable property	200	–
Immovable property	100	100
Gross estate	300	100
Deduction of debts	–60	–
Net estate	240	100
Rate of tax (in per cent)	30	40
Tax	72	40

Taxation under the Convention:

State B may, under Article 5, tax the immovable property	100
It has, under paragraph 1, to deduct the debt	–60
And taxes the net estate	40
At 40%, that is	16

77

State A has to allocate the debt also to the immovable property, the net value of which is now 40:

a) If State A uses the exemption method it has to exempt the 40; thus taxing only 200 at a rate of 30%;

b) If State A uses the credit method it has to give credit against its own tax for the tax levied in State B, but the credit may not exceed that part of its own tax which is attributable to the net amount of the immovable property, that is, 30% of 40. State A has, under the Convention, to grant a credit of 12.

Should the domestic law of State A grant a more favourable treatment, State A may have to apply its domestic law (see also paragraphs 37 *et seq.* below).

18. *EXAMPLE 2* (to paragraph 3)

The deceased died domiciled in State A. His estate consists of:

Movable property	200
Immovable property situated in State B	100
Gross estate	300
A debt which has no economic connection with any of the assets of the estate	−60
Net estate	240

When taxing as a State of *situs,* State B grants, under domestic law, a proportional deduction of the debts of the estate.

Taxation under domestic law:

	State A	State B
Movable property	200	–
Immovable property	100	100
Gross estate	300	100
Deduction of debts	−60	−20
Net estate	240	80
Rate of tax (in per cent)	30	40
Tax	72	32

Taxation under the Convention:

State B may tax the immovable property, but under paragraph 3, it need not deduct the debt	100
The tax is (40% of 100)	40

State A has to allocate the debt against the movable property. The net value of the immovable property situated in State B is therefore 100.

a) If State A uses the exemption method it has to exempt from its tax base of 240 the net value of the immovable property, 100. It may tax 140 at a rate of 30%;

b) If State A uses the credit method it has to credit against its own tax of 72 the tax levied in State B attributable to the net value of the immovable property, that is, 30% of 100. State A therefore grants a credit of 30.

19.   *EXAMPLE 3* (to paragraph 3)

The deceased died domiciled in State A. State B, under its domestic law, adopts the proportional method for the deduction of debts. The estate consists of:

Movable property situated in State A	60
Immovable property situated in State B	200
Immovable property in a third State (no convention with States A and B)	140
Gross estate	400
A debt economically connected with the immovable property situated in the third State (see paragraph 1)	−150
Net estate	250

State A, under its domestic law, allocates the foreign debt to foreign property.

Taxation under domestic law:

	State A	State B
Movable property	60	–
Immovable property in State B	200	200
Immovable property in a third State	140	–
Gross estate	400	200
Deduction of debts	−150	−75
Net estate	250	125
Rate of tax (in per cent)	30	40
Tax	75	50

Taxation under the Convention:

State B taxes the immovable property situated in its territory	200

But under paragraph 3 it needs not deduct any debts from this property.

The tax is (40% of 200)	80

State A already has to deduct the debt of 150 under domestic law from the value of the immovable property siuated in the third State (140). Under paragraph 3, and contrary to its domestic law, State A has to deduct the excess of 10 from the value of the movable property (60). The net estate of 250 in State A therefore includes 200 which may be taxed in State B.

a)   If State A uses the exemption method it has to exempt 200 from its tax base of 250 and it may tax 50 at a rate of 30%;

b)   If State A uses the credit method it has to give credit against its own tax for the tax levied in State B, but the credit may not exceed that part of its own tax which is attributable to the property which may be taxed in State B. The credit may therefore not exceed 30% of 200, that is, 60.

Paragraph 4

20.   Paragraphs 1 and 2 provide for a deduction of certain debts from the value of certain assets on which they are secured, or with which they are economically connected. The debts in question, however, may exceed the value of the property from which they

have to be deducted under those paragraphs. Paragraph 4 provides, as a special rule for such cases, that the excess of such debts has then to be deducted from the value of other property which may be taxed in the same State.

21.   *EXAMPLE 4* (to paragraphs 1 and 4)

The deceased died domiciled in State A. His estate consists of:

Two items of immovable property situated in State B each worth 100	200
Movable property	300
Gross estate	500
A debt economically connected with the first item of immovable property (see paragraph 1)	−150
Net estate	350

When taxing as a State of *situs*, State B allows no deduction for debts under its domestic law.

Taxation under domestic law:

	State A	State B
Movable property	300	–
Immovable property	200	200
Gross estate	500	200
Deduction of debts	−150	–
Net estate	350	200
Rate of tax (in percent)	30	40
Tax	105	80

Taxation under the Convention

State B may tax both items of immovable property	200
Under paragraph 1 it has to deduct the debt of 150 from the value of the property (100) with which it is connected, leaving an excess of 50. Under paragraph 4, State B has to deduct that excess from the value of the second item of immovable property; the deduction is therefore	−150
Net estate	50
The tax is (40% of 50)	20

State A has to allocate the debt in the same way, and therefore also attributes a net value of 50 to the immovable property which may be taxed in State B.

a)   If State A uses the exemption method it excludes from its tax base of 350 that net value of 50 and taxes 300 at a rate of 30%.

b)   If State A uses the credit method it has to give credit against its own tax for the tax levied in State B, but the credit may not exceed that part of its own tax which is attributable to the net value of the property which may be taxed in the other State, or 30% of 50, that is, 15.

Paragraph 5

22.   This paragraph follows the principle that, regarded as a whole, only the net estate (neither more nor less) should be taxed in the two Contracting States.

23.   The rules of Articles 5 to 7 deal with an attribution of the right to tax the various types of assets. The provisions of paragraphs to 4 of Article 8 follow the same pattern. In total, the taxation rights given to the Contracting States by Articles 5 to 7 should, as a result of paragraphs 1 to 4 of Article 8, be confined to the net value of the estate.

24.   In some cases, however, the rules of paragraphs 1 to 4 may lead to the result that the debts allocated to one State exceed the value of the property which, under the Convention, is taxable in that State. Paragraph 5 aims to cover such cases by transferring the deductibility of such an excess to property which is taxable in the other State. The following examples illustrate the effects of paragraph 5:

25.   *EXAMPLE 5*

> The deceased died domiciled in State A. His estate consists of immovable property situated in State B worth 100 and movable property worth 200. There is a debt of 150 economically connected with the immovable property (paragraph 1).
>
> The application of the rules of Article 5 and of paragraphs 1 and 4 of Article 8 would lead to the result that State B would have to deduct the debt of 150 from the value of the immovable property (100) situated in its territory which leaves a deficit of 50. State A, if it uses the exemption method, would have the right to tax the movable property of 200. However, since there is in State B an excess of debts of 50, State A has to deduct that excess from the value of the movable property, thus taxing only 150.

26.   *EXAMPLE 6*

> The deceased died domiciled in State A. His estate consists solely of immovable property situated in State B of 200 and there is a debt, not connected with that property, of 150.
>
> Under Article 5, *State B* may tax the immovable property. Under paragraph 3, the debt of 150, not having a special economic connection, should be deducted from the property falling under Article 7. However, since there is no property falling under Article 7, paragraph 5 requires that the debt be deducted from the immovable property in State B. Consequently, State B may impose its tax on a net estate of $200 - 150 = 50$.
>
> *a)*   If *State A* uses the exemption method it has to exempt the immovable property thus its tax base is reduced to nil.
>
> *b)*   If State A uses the credit method it may impose its tax on the total net estate, that is, on $200 - 150 = 50$, but it has to give credit for State B's tax on 50. Assuming State A's rate of tax is 36% and State B's rate of tax is 28%, the tax assessed in State A will be:

36% of 50	18
Credit for State B's tax (28% of 50)	−14
Tax in State A	4

27.   Paragraph 5 has to be interpreted, however, in a way which ensures that no advantages or disadvantages may arise for the taxpayer.

28.   In the application of that paragraph due regard should be had to the fact that the amount of an excess of debts incurred under the application of the law of one State may be different from the amount determined under the law of the other State. Article 8 does not require a Contracting State to deduct an excess of debts which arises in the other Contracting State solely by reason of special rules, for example, of valuation, applied in that other State.

29.   Problems may frequently arise, for example, in the case of land used for agricultural purposes. Many countries allow for domestic agricultural land a valuation (so-called "tax value") which differs widely from its actual value. The following examples illustrate this point:

30.   *EXAMPLE 7*

The deceased died domiciled in State A. His estate consists of immovable property situated in State B, the real value of which is 200 but the tax value, according to the law of State B, is 100. There is a debt connected with that property of 150 (paragraph 1). The movable assets of the estate amount to 250.

State B taxes the immovable property on a value of 100 and deducts therefrom the debt of 150 which gives a deficit of 50.

State A could, under its domestic law, tax the whole of the estate (450) less the debt (150).

a)   If State A uses the exemption method it has now to exempt the immovable property (200) less the debt (150). There is no need to deduct the excess of the debt (50) in State B.

b)   If State A uses the credit method it will have already deducted the full amount of the debt in arriving at its tax base of 300. There is no necessity for it to deduct an additional 50 arising solely because of the special valuation rules of State B.

31.   *EXAMPLE 8*

The facts are the same as in Example 7, except that the debt connected with the immovable property is 250 (paragraph 1).

There now arises in State B an excess of debts of 150.

a)   If State A uses the credit method it will have already deducted the whole of the debt so there is no need to deduct a further excess of debts arising in State B.

b)   If State A uses the exemption method it will exempt the immovable property of 200 and will, under paragraphs 1 and 4, limit the deduction of the debt connected therewith also to 200. Of the total deficit in State B amounting to 150, 50 has not so far been deducted in State A. As a result of paragraph 5, State A has now to deduct an additional 50.

Paragraph 6

32.   Article 8 places on each Contracting State the obligation to deduct, to the extent prescribed by the Article, the deceased person's debts against that part of the estate which it taxes.

33.   The rules of Article 8, as already indicated, work in two directions:

    i)   they sometimes require a State to deduct, according to the economic link of a debt with certain property included within the estate, debts which, under its domestic law, would not be deductible; and

    ii) in other situations they give a State the right to decline the deduction of debts which, under its domestic law, would be deductible.

34.   These rules should work satisfactorily in cases where both States can apply the Article in both ways. Should any State, because of its domestic law, be unable to exercise its right under Article 8 to decline to deduct debts, Article 8 may lead to a double deduction of debts not envisaged by the Convention, as shown in the following example:

35.   *EXAMPLE 9*

The deceased died domiciled in State A. His estate consists of immovable property situated in State B worth 100 and movable property worth 100. There is a debt of 40 economically connected with the immovable property (see paragraph 1).

Under the Convention, State B should tax the immovable property (100) less the debt (40) that is, an amount of 60. State A, if it uses the exemption method, should exempt that immovable property (100) and take no account of the debt connected with the property (40), which leaves that State with a taxable estate of 100.

It may, however, happen that State A, under its domestic law, can follow the Convention as far as the exemption of the immovable property is concerned, but will not be able to follow the Convention as far as the exclusion of the debt is concerned. That leaves State A with a tax base of 60.

The net result is that the debt of 40 would have been deducted twice. That result cannot be avoided if State B is required, under its domestic law, to deduct that debt notwithstanding Article 8.

36.   Where, however, the debt mentioned in paragraph 35 would become deductible in State B solely by reason of paragraph 1, paragraph 6 provides that State B would not have to deduct that debt under such circumstances.

37.   *EXAMPLE 10*

The deceased died domiciled in State A. His estate consists of:

Movable property	100
Immovable property situated in State B	100
Gross estate	200
A debt economically connected with the immovable property (see paragraph 1)	–40
Net estate	160

State A uses the credit method for unilateral relief from double taxation and allocates its tax on the foreign property in the same ratio as the value of such property bears to the gross value of the estate (in the present case 1 : 2).

State B, when taxing as a country of *situs,* does not allow the deduction of any debts.

Taxation under domestic law

	State A	State B
Movable property	100	–
Immovable property	100	100
Gross estate	200	100
Deduction of debts	–40	–
Net estate	160	100
Rate of tax (in per cent)	30	40
Tax	48	40
Credit for foreign tax (30% of $\frac{160}{2}$)	–24	–
Net tax	24	40

Taxation under the Convention

State B taxes the immovable property	100
And deducts, under paragraph 1, the debt	–40
Net estate in State B	60
The tax is 40% of 60	24

State A allocates the debt to the immovable property and gives relief under Articles 9A or 9B for the net value of 60.

a) If State A uses the exemption method it exempts from its tax base of 160 the net value of the immovable property (60) and therefore taxes 100 at 30 per cent, that is, 30
which is higher than the tax due when unilateral relief is given

b) If State A uses the credit method, it credits against its tax of 48 the tax paid in State B up to 30% of the net value of the immovable property, that is, 30% of 60 –18

The tax collected in State A would then be which is also higher than the tax due when unilateral relief is given 30

38.   If, in this example, State A has to apply its domestic law, paragraph 6 takes away from State B the obligation to deduct debts deducted in State A.

39.   Contrary to its domestic law, State B had to deduct, under paragraph 1, the debt of 40. If, contrary to paragraph 1, State A is required under its domestic law to deduct part of the debt from property falling under Article 7, paragraph 6 removes to that extent the obligation of State B to deduct the debt. By applying its domestic law State A has allocated half of that debt against the value of the movable property. State B is entitled, under paragraph 6, to refuse the deduction of the debt to the same extent. State B will tax therefore 100 – 20 = 80 at a rate of 40%, that is, 32.

B. States taxing on a subsidiary basis of nationality or other like criteria

40.   If the Contracting States reserve the right to tax on the basis of nationality in conformity with paragraph 6 of the Commentary on Article 7, then they must complete paragraph 3 of Article 8 with a reference to the provision for taxation by the State of nationality; paragraph 5 of Article 8 must then be understood as also being capable of application to such a State. The same applies to taxation on any of the other bases mentioned in paragraph 72 of the Commentary on Articles 9A and 9B or on the basis of domicile (within the meaning of the domestic law) in conformity with paragraph 12 of the Commentary on Article 4.

C. Meaning of "debts"

41.   Article 8 does not give a definition of what is to be regarded as a deductible debt. Since it is the aim of the Article to link the division of the taxation rights which the two Contracting States may have under their domestic laws, with a corresponding rule for the division of debts, so that, in effect, the taxation rights relate to the net estate, the question whether a certain obligation is to be regarded as a deductible debt has, in the first instance, to be decided under the domestic law of each Contracting State.

42.   It is not intended that article 8 should enlarge the scope of the domestic laws of the Contracting States as to what constitutes a deductible debt. An obligation which would not, under any circumstances, be regarded as a deductible debt in a Contracting State will not become deductible simply by the provisions of the Article. This holds true even if such a debt is deductible under the law of the other Contracting State.

43.   *EXAMPLE 11*

The deceased died domiciled in State A. His estate consists of:

Movable property	100
Immovable property situated in State B	200
Gross estate	300
And a debt, the nature of which is explained in the different cases	−120
Net estate	180

The rate of tax is 30% in State A and 25% in State B

First case

The debt is not deductible in either Contracting State (for example, repair work on a building situated in State B was financed by a loan from the deceased's brother; there exists a written document vouching that debt, but under the domestic laws of both Contracting States a debt owed to a close relative is recognised only if evidenced before a notary public).

Under paragraph 1, the debt must be allocated to the immovable property situated in State B. This provision, however, does not make it deductible if it is not deductible under the domestic laws of the two States.

State B therefore may tax that property on the gross amount of 200 at 25%. State A, when using the exemption method, exempts from its tax base of 300 the gross amount of the immovable property of 200. If State A uses the credit method it taxes the estate on 300 at 30% and gives credit for State B's tax in an amount of 50.

44. *Second case*

The debt is deductible only under the domestic law of one State (for example, repair work on a building situated in State B was financed by a loan from the deceased's brother; there exists a written document vouching that debt; under the law of State A such a debt would be recognised, but under the law of State B a debt owed to a close relative is recognised only if evidenced before a notary public).

Under paragraph 1, the debt must be allocated to the immovable property situated in State B. This provision, however, does not make it deductible, if it is not deductible under the domestic law of that State. State B therefore taxes the immovable property on the gross amount of 200 at 25%, amounting to 50.

State A, when using the exemption method, exempts from its tax base (180) the net value of the immovable property (80) and taxes 100 at 30%. State A will, therefore, exempt only the net value of the immovable property, although that property was taxed in State B on the gross value thereof.

In State A uses the credit method it taxes the estate on 180 at 30%. From the resulting tax of 54 State A has to deduct as credit for State B's tax 24 (30% of 80). State A will therefore give credit for State B's tax on the gross value of the immovable property in State B but the credit is limited to the amount of its own tax on the net value of that property.

45.   Article 8 aims only at a justifiable division of the taxation rights between the two Contracting States over what each State would, in principle, regard as the net estate. This is illustrated in the following cases.

46. *Third case*

At the time of death a bill for repair work done on a building in State B is still unsettled. State A (State of the deceased's domicile) would deduct such a debt in any case. State B would deduct such a debt only if the deceased was domiciled at the time of death in its territory, that is, only if a comprehensive tax liability is imposed; if State B taxes only as State of *situs* (limited tax liability) it deducts no debts at all. This debt has to be deducted in State B under paragraph 1, since it is the sort of debt which would be deductible if State B were imposing a comprehensive tax liability.

47. *Fourth case*

At the time of death a bill for repair work done on a building is still unsettled. Both Contracting States recognise this as a deductible debt, but both of them deduct debts only in the same ratio as the estate taxable in their country bears to the whole of the estate.

Under paragraph 1, the full amount of the debt must be deducted in State B. If State A used the exemption method, it refrains from deducting the debt. If State A uses the credit method, it will give credit for the tax of State B against its own tax on the net value of the immovable property situated in State B.

D. Legacies

48.   Article 9 relates only to debts incurred by the deceased. It does not deal with the treatment of pecuniary legacies given by the deceased. The treatment of such legacies may be different under the domestic laws of two Contracting States. States which levy an estate tax will impose tax on the deceased's estate without regard to the persons to whom the property is transferred. States which levy inheritance taxes will impose their tax on the separate transfers to the different heirs or legatees.

49. *EXAMPLE 12*

The deceased died domiciled in State A. His estate consists solely of immovable property of 1,000 situated in State B. His sole heir is his son but a pecuniary legacy of 400 is given to his wife.

A State levying an estate tax will tax the 1,000 as immovable property, whereas a State which levies an inheritance tax may tax the legatee on an amount of 400, which it may or may not regard as immovable property, and then tax the heir on a net amount of 600 which it regards as immovable property.

50. If, under the rules of Articles 5 to 7, the right to tax the property taken both by the heir and by the legatee is attributed to the same State, the Convention works satisfactorily. If, however, one State regarded the property as falling under Article 5 and the other under Article 7, the result would be either unrelieved double taxation or double non-taxation.

51. States which levy an estate tax will not lose under the Convention their right to tax immovable property situated in their territories if pecuniary legacies are paid out of that property.

52. States which levy inheritances taxes could, however, lose under the Convention the right to tax immovable property situated in their territories if, under their domestic laws, a pecuniary legacy paid out of immovable property would be regarded as property falling under Article 7. Where this is the case some States may be able to find a solution to this problem by providing in their bilateral conventions that pecuniary legacies paid out of property falling under Article 5 or 6 shall be regarded as falling under those Articles and not under Article 7.

OBSERVATION ON THE COMMENTARY

53. *Spain* observes that the Spanish legislation distinguishes as between "debts" (which decrease the value of the property but do not affect it) and "charges" (rights which directly affect the Property).

RESERVATIONS ON THE ARTICLE

54. *New Zealand, Portugal,* the *United Kingdom* and the *United States* note that their domestic laws do not allow them to give effect to this Article and therefore wish to reserve their positions.

COMMENTARY ON ARTICLES 9A AND 9B CONCERNING METHODS FOR ELIMINATING DOUBLE TAXATION

I. PRELIMINARY REMARKS

A. Taxes on the occasion of death

General Observations

1.   There are a number of situations where international double taxation may arise in two States on the occasion of death, for example, where:

  a)   the deceased was domiciled in one State under its domestic law and in the other State under its own domestic law;

  b)   the deceased was domiciled in one State but was a national of the other State;

  c)   the deceased was domiciled in one State but the heir was either domiciled in, or a national of, the other State;

  d)   the deceased was domiciled in one State but part or all of his property was situated in the other State;

  e)   the deceased was a national of one State but part or all of his property was situated in the other State;

  f)   the deceased was a national of one State but the heir was domiciled in, or a national of, the other State;

  g)   neither the deceased nor the heir was domiciled in, or a national of, one of the States but the same property is, under the domestic law of each State, deemed to be situated within its territory.

2.   Only the conflicts in cases *a), b), c)* and *d)* above come within the scope of the Convention: this is because it does not apply unless the deceased, at the time of his death, was domiciled in one or both of the Contracting States. As regards *e), f)* and, in some cases even *g)*, see paragraphs 5 and 6 of the Commentary on Article 1.

3.   The conflict in cases *a), b)* and *c)* is reduced by the Convention to the case of *d);* only the State in which the deceased person was domiciled within the meaning of the Convention may impose a comprehensive tax liability. The other State loses any comprehensive tax charge which it may have under its domestic law and can tax only property falling under Articles 5 and 6.

4.   The double taxation which occurs when the deceased, domiciled within the meaning of the Convention in one Contracting State, leaves property taxable in the other [the case falling under *d)* of paragraph 1 above] may be resolved by having either the State of domicile or the other State (the State of *situs*) relinquish the right to tax.

Where the State of *situs* relinquishes its right to tax, the relevant Article provides that the property "shall be taxable only" in the State where the deceased died domiciled (Article 7); accordingly no question of double taxation arises here. Where, on the other hand, the State of *situs* retains its right to tax, that is, where the relevant Article provides that the property "may be taxed" in that State (Articles 5 and 6), which does not exclude taxation by the State of domicile, the latter State must give relief so as to avoid double taxation. This is the aim of Articles 9A and 9B.

Description of Methods for Eliminating Double Taxation

5.　　In existing conventions, two leading principles are followed for eliminating double taxation by the State in which the deceased was domiciled.

1. *The principle of exemption*

6.　　Under the principle of exemption, the State where the deceased died domiciled does not tax the property which, according to the Convention, may be taxed in the other State (State of *situs*).

7.　　The principle of exemption may be applied by two main methods:

a) The property which may be taxed in the State of *situs* is not taken into account at all by the State of domicile for the purposes of its tax. The State of domicile is not entitled to take the property so exempted into consideration when determining the rate of tax to be imposed on the rest of the estate. This method is called "full exemption";

b) The property which may be taxed in the State of *situs* is not taxed in the State of domicile, but the State of domicile retains the right to take it into consideration when determining the rate of tax to be imposed on the rest of the estate. This method is called "exemption with progression".

2. *The principle of credit*

8.　　Under the principle of credit, the State in which the deceased died domiciled calculates its tax on the total estate or inheritance including the property which, under the Convention, may be taxed in the State of *situs*. It then allows a deduction from its own tax for the tax paid in the State of *situs*.

9.　　The principle of credit may be applied by two main methods:

a) The State of domicile allows the deduction of the total amount of tax paid in the State of *situs* on property which may be taxed in the State of *situs;* this method is called "full credit";

b) The deduction given by the State of domicile for the tax paid in the State of *situs* is restricted to that part of its own tax which is attributable to the property which may be taxed in the State of *situs;* this method is called "ordinary credit".

10.　　Fundamentally, the difference between the principles is that the exemption principle looks at the property to be taxed, while the credit principle looks at the tax.

3. *Operation and effects of the methods*

11.   The operation and the effects of the various methods are explained in detail in paragraphs 18 to 27 of the Commentaries on Articles 23A and 23B of the 1977 Income Tax Model.

4. *Methods proposed in Articles 9A and 9B*

12.   In the conventions concluded between OECD Member countries each of the leading principles has been accepted: some States have a preference for exemption, others for credit. While a single principle might theoretically be more desirable, the present Model allows each State to choose the principle to apply in order to take account of those preferences, customs or the particular features of its law.

13.   On the other hand, it has been found important to limit the number of methods to be employed with respect to each leading principle. In view of this limitation, the Articles have been drafted so that Member countries are left free to choose between two methods:

- the exemption method with progression (Article 9A), and
- the ordinary credit method (Article 9B).

14.   If two Contracting States adopt the same method, it will be sufficient to insert the relevant Article in their convention. On the other hand, if the two States adopt different methods, both methods must be included in their convention; they may be amalgamated into one Article, each part of the Article stating clearly to which State it applies.

15.   The two Articles are drafted in general terms and do not give detailed rules on how the exemption or credit is to be computed, this being left to the domestic laws and practice of the States concerned. States which find it necessary to settle any problem in their convention are free to do so in bilateral negotiations.

B.   Taxes on life-time gifts

16.   It has been noted that the scope of the Convention has been extended to cover taxes on life-time gifts. Where tax is imposed on the same event in both Contracting States, the Convention operates to relieve double taxation arising on life-time gifts in the same way as it operates to relieve the double taxation of estates or inheritances. All the remarks made above relating to death duties apply therefore, *mutatis mutandis,* to taxes on gifts.

C.   Interrelation between death duties (or gift taxes) and taxes imposed on a previous gift

17.   Many OECD Member countries, when imposing death duties or gift taxes, take into account previous gifts. Where this goes further than the inclusion of the previous gift for the purpose of progressivity of the tax due by reason of the new event, some part of the tax which is then imposed may be attributable to the earlier gift. Since that gift, at the time when it was made, may have been subject to a gift tax in the other State, international double taxation may arise because taxes were levied on the same property on two different events. An example may illustrate this:

18. *EXAMPLE 1*

The deceased died domiciled in State A. His estate consists of movable property of 400. During his life-time he made a gift to his son, his sole heir, of immovable property worth 100 situated in State B. At the time of the gift, the gift was subject to a gift tax in State A of 15 and in State B of 30. At the time of death, State A includes that previous gift in its death duty assessment in the following way:

It taxes the estate, including the gift, on a value of	500
at a rate of, say, 40%	200
State A, under its domestic law, gives relief for its own gift taxes which were formely imposed on that gift, say[1]	– 15
The estate tax amounts to	185

Part of State A's death duties $(40 – 15 = 25)$ is attributable to the immovable property in State B. Since that gift has borne gift tax in State B at the time of the gift, international double taxation arises in addition to that which arose at the time of the gift.

19.   It was thought desirable to provide, in this Convention, rules for the avoidance of such international double taxation (see paragraph 2 of Articles 9A and 9B). Member countries which, on the one hand, want to include taxes on life-time gifts within their conventions, but which, on the other hand, do not want to deal with international double taxation as a result of taxes on two different events, can do so by keeping death duties and gift taxes separate in their bilateral conventions in the same way as income and capital taxes are kept separate in Article 23 of the 1977 Income Tax Model (see paragraph 1 of Article 23B).

II. COMMENTARY ON THE PROVISIONS OF ARTICLE 9A
(EXEMPTION METHOD)

20.   Paragraph 1 of this Article deals with the exemption to be given by the State of the deceased's or the donor's domicile for property which forms part of the estate or the gift (elimination of double taxation arising from taxation in relation to the same event). Paragraph 2 deals with the exemption which must be given for property which has been the subject of a previous gift and which is included within the assessment of death duties or of gift tax on the occasion of a later gift. Paragraph 3 preserves the right of the State of domicile to take account of the exempted property in determining the rate of tax on the property which it may tax.

Paragraph 1

A. The obligation of the State of domicile to give exemption

21.   In the Article it is laid down that the State of domicile shall exempt from tax, property which, under the Convention, "may be taxed" in the other State (State of *situs*).

---

1.   The form in which such a relief is given varies under the domestic laws of Member countries. Some give credit for the actual tax paid at the time of the previous gift, others give credit for a notional amount of tax, calculated as if the gift had ben made at the time of death. Examples given in this Commentary assume that credit is given for the actual tax paid at the time of the gift.

22.   The State of domicile must, accordingly, give exemption whether or not the property in question is taxed in the State of *situs*. This is so, in particular, in cases where the State of *situs* does not effectively levy tax on the property owing to some special circumstance such as, for example, the operation of a relief, an omission or a mistake made by an official, the operation of a statutory time limit. This method is certainly the most practical since it relieves the State of domicile from undertaking investigations of the actual tax position in the State of *situs*.

23.   If the domestic law of the State of *situs* does not entitle it to make full use of the right to tax reserved to it by the Convention, then in order to avoid double non-taxation, Contracting States may find it reasonable in certain circumstances to make an exception to the obligation on the State of domicile to give exemption. In such cases it is left to States, in their bilateral negotiations, to agree upon the necessary modifications to the Article. Conversely, an exception might also be possible in order to preserve the right of the State of *situs* to tax other property in addition to that falling under Articles 5 and 6 if the State of domicile is not entitled by its law to tax such other property.

24.   Since it exempts the property which may be taxed in the State of *situs,* the State of domicile is entitled, subject to the provisions of paragraph 5 of Article 8, to disregard all debts which, according to paragraphs 1, 2 and 4 of Article 8, must in the first instance be deducted from the property taxable in the State of *situs*.

25.   The value of the property to be exempted from tax by the State of domicile is the amount which, but for the Convention, would be subject to its estate, inheritance or gift tax according to its domestic law. This value may differ from the amount subject to tax in the State of *situs* according to its domestic law.

B.   Treatment of special deductions

26.   Difficulties may arise because the laws of most States provide for special deductions from the net amount of the estate or gift, or from specific items of the estate or gift, on the relationship between the deceased or the donor and the heir, legatee, or donee.

The following example illustrates these difficulties:

EXAMPLE 2

The surviving spouse has inherited all the property left by the deceased. The estate consists of:

a)	Net estate falling under Article 7	200
b)	Net estate falling under Article 5	100
c)	Total net estate	300
d)	A special deduction granted under the law of the State of domicile for inheritances between spouses	– 60
	Estate subject to tax	240

The question is, what amount should be exempted from tax in the State of domicile; several answers are possible, for example:

– 100 (item b), leaving a taxable amount of 140;
– 80 (one third of item e, according to ratio between item b and item c) leaving a taxable amount of 160;
– 40 (item b less item d) leaving a taxable amount of 200 (full amount of item a).

27.   A comparison of the laws and practices of Member countries shows that the answer to this question varies considerably from country to country, especially in countries which impose an inheritance tax and where the tax-free amounts (item d of Example 2 above) vary between the different heirs and legatees. The amount of such allowances may also depend on the kind of property involved (for example, special allowances for the home of the deceased and his family). The solution adopted by a State will depend on the general principles of its tax system and on its tax structure. It may be the intention of a State of domicile that the persons domiciled therein enjoy the full benefit of such deductions. In other States these tax-free amounts are apportioned.

28.   In view of the wide variety of fiscal law and practice in the different States regarding the determination of tax, especially in relation to deductions, allowances and similar benefits, it is preferable not to propose an express and uniform solution in the Convention, but to leave each State free to apply its own law and practice. States which prefer to have a special problem solved in their conventions are free to do so in bilateral negotiations. Finally, the question is also of importance for States applying the credit method (see paragraph 57 below).

Paragraph 2

The obligation to give exemption for previous gifts

29.   Since taxes on life-term gifts have been included within the scope of the Convention, paragraph 2 provides a rule for the avoidance of double taxation which may arise when one State taxes property which was taxed in the other State on the occasion of a previous gift (see paragraph 17 above).

30.   Under this rule, the State of domicile must give exemption for property included in its assessment which was the subject of a previous gift and which, at the time of the gift, may have been taxed in the other State in accordance with the provisions of the Convention. This rule is illustrated by the following examples where it is assumed that both Contracting States include previous gifts in the assessment of death duties and that the Convention was applicable on both events. This rule applies, not only where the later event is the death of the donor, but also where it is a later gift made by him.

31.   *First case:*   Between the time of the gift and the time of his death, the donor remained domiciled in the same State.

EXAMPLE 3 (domicile unchanged)

The donor was at the time of the gift and the time of his death domiciled in State A. He made a gift to his son of:

Movable property	100
Immovable property situated in State B	200

He died three years later. His sole heir is his son.

The estate consists of:

Movable property	700
Immovable property situated in State B	800

The Convention produces the following results (as to the application of progressivity in State B, see paragraph 38 below).

i) *At the time of the gift:*

State B may tax the immovable property situated in its territory	200
State A has the exclusive taxation right on the movable property	100

It has to give exemption with progression (see paragraph 3) for the immovable property situated in State B.

ii) *At the time of death:*

State B may tax the immovable property forming part of the estate and situated in its territory	800
It includes within its assessment the immovable property situated in its territory which formed part of the previous gift	200
State A has the exclusive taxation right on the movable property forming part of the estate	700
And it has the exclusive right to include that part of the previous gift consisting of movable property	100

Under paragraph 1, State A has to give exemption (with progression) for the immovable property which is part of the estate and which is situated in State B (800). Similarly, under paragraph 2, it must exempt, subject to progression, the previous gift which consists of immovable property situated in State B (200).

32. *Second case:* Between the time of the gift and the time of his death, the donor changed his domicile from one Contracting State to the other.

EXAMPLE 4 (domicile changed from one Contracting State to the other)

While domiciled in State B the donor made a gift to his son of:

Movable property	100
Immovable property situated in State B	200

Subsequently he changed his domicile to State A and died domiciled there three years later. His sole heir is his son. The estate consists of:

Movable property	700
Immovable property situated in State B	800

The Convention produces the following result (as to the application of progressivity in State B, see paragraph 38 below):

i) *At the time of the gift:*

State B has the exclusive taxation right on the whole of the gift	300

ii) *At the time of death:*

State B may tax the immovable property, forming part of the estate and situated in its territory	800
It may include within this assessment only that part of the previous gift consisting of immovable property situated in its territory	200
State A has the exclusive taxation right on the movable property forming part of the estate	700

It has to give exemption with progression (see paragraph 3) for the immovable property which forms part of the estate and is situated in State B (paragraph 1)   800

Similarly, under paragraph 2, it must exempt, subject to progression, the previous gift   300

33.   The exemption to be given under paragraph 2 does not, however, apply to property falling under Articles 5 and 6 which is situated in the State of domicile of the deceased and which formed part of a former gift. The reason for this limitation is that the country of *situs* should always be entitled to full taxation rights in respect of such property. This limitation is illustrated by the following example.

EXAMPLE 5   (domicile changed from one Contracting State to the other)

While domiciled in State B the donor made a gift to his son of:

Movable property	100
Immovable property situated in State A	200

Subsequently he changed his domicile to State A and died domiciled there three years later. His sole heir is his son. The estate consists of:

Movable property	700
Immovable property situated in State B	800

State A uses the exemption method and State B the credit method for the avoidance of double taxation.

The Convention produces the following result:

i)   *At the time of the gift:*

State A taxes the immovable property situated in its territory	200	
At 5%		10
State B taxes the whole gift	300	
At 20%		60
And gives credit for State A's tax		– 10
It imposes a net tax		50

And has thereby levied a tax according to the Convention on the immovable property situated in State A of 30 (20% of 200 = 40 less credit of 10);

ii)   *At the time of death:*

State B taxes only the immovable property situated in its territory   800

And is not entitled to include any part of the previous gift within this assessment.

State A has the exclusive taxation right on the movable property, which is part of the estate   700

It has to give exemption (with progression, see paragraph 3) for the immovable property which is situated in State B   800

> As to the inclusion of the previous gift, the whole of which has been taxed in State B according to the Convention at the time of the gift, State A has, under paragraph 2, to give no relief for that part which is immovable property situated in its own territory. State A may therefore include that part of the previous gift (200) within its assessment. The remaining part of the gift (that is, movable property of 100) may be included only for the purposes of progressivity.

34. It has to be admitted that, in the case dealt with in Example 5 above, there remains a certain amount of double taxation of the kind illustrated in paragraph 18 above. It was decided, however, that, in such rare cases, the full taxation right of the State of *situs* of property falling under Articles 5 and 6 should be safeguarded. States which wish to give relief in such circumstances are free to do so either by deleting the last part of paragraph 2 or by providing for State A to give credit for State B's tax.

35. Paragraph 2 applies only to property which has been taxed "in accordance with the provisions of the Convention". It does not apply therefore if the previous gift was not covered by the Convention (for example, because the Convention entered into force at a later date, or because, at the time of the gift, the donor was not domiciled in either Contracting State). States which want to extend the scope of this paragraph to cover cases of this kind may do so, in bilateral negotiations, by replacing the words "in accordance with the provisions of the Convention" by the words "not contrary to the provisions of the Convention".

36. In cases where the Convention was applicable at the time of the gift but not at the time of death or the later gift (for example, because of the termination of the Convention or a change of domicile by the donor from one Contracting State to a third State), some States may want the Convention to continue to have effect (to preserve the relief given by the Convention at the time of the earlier gift) in respect of assets included in the assessment of the estate or the later gift which formed part of a gift made at a time when the Convention was applicable. They are free to insert a special provision to this effect in bilateral negotiations.

Paragraph 3

The reservation of the progression

37. In most of the conventions concluded between Member countries on the basis of the exemption method, the State of domicile retains the right to take the exempted property into account when determining the rate of tax to be imposed on the rest of the estate. The Article gives effect to this by providing in paragraph 3 that the State of domicile may apply the rate which would be applicable if the property in question had not been exempted under paragraphs 1 or 2.

38. The question of preserving the progressive tax rate may also arise for the State which is not the State of domicile even though the Convention limits the taxation right of that State to property falling under Articles 5 and 6. This may happen for a number of reasons: because the domestic law of that State provides for a progressive tax rate by reference to the total value of all taxable property situated in its territory, or even by reference to the total value of the estate or gift, or when, in the absence of the Convention, that State would have had the right to tax the total estate or gift and, consequently, at the rate of tax appropriate to that total (such a situation is most likely to

occur in those States which have a comprehensive right to tax on the basis of the nationality of the deceased or donor or the domicile or nationality of the heir). The Article does not prejudice the application by the State of *situs* of its domestic law provisions on progressivity. If two States wish to determine whether and to what extent the State of *situs* may apply progressive rates they are free to do so in their bilateral negotiations.

III.   COMMENTARY ON THE PROVISIONS OF ARTICLE 9B
(CREDIT METHOD)

39.   Paragraph 1 of this Article deals with the credit to be given by the State of the deceased's or the donor's domicile for the tax on property which forms part of the estate or the gift (elimination of double taxation arising from taxation in relation to the same event). Paragraph 2 deals with the credit which must be given for the tax on property which has been the subject of a previous gift and which is included within the assessment of death duties or of gift tax on the occasion of a later gift. Paragraph 3 deals with the limitations under which the credit under paragraphs 1 and 2 is to be given.

Paragraph 1

Credit to be given by the State of domicile

40.   Article 9B, based on the credit principle, follows the ordinary credit method: the State of domicile allows as a deduction from its own tax on the estate of, or the gift made by, the person domiciled in its territory an amount equal to the tax paid in the other State on the property which, under the provisions of the Convention, may be taxed in that other State, but the deduction is restricted to the appropriate proportion of its own tax attributable to such property.

41.   In each Contracting State the tax in respect of any particular item or items of property must be computed subject to any abatements, reductions for family responsibilities or other benefits provided by the domestic law.

42.   The text of Article 9B means, in particular, that the deduction allowed by the State of domicile on the property which may be taxed in the other State is to be restricted to the amount of tax effectively paid in the other State, even if the other State has allowed a deduction from its own tax for tax paid on the same property in some third State, whether under its domestic law or under a convention concluded with the third State. Suppose, for example, that a deceased domiciled in State A had in State B a permanent establishment, the assets of which included, *inter alia,* property taxed in State C. Between State B and State C there is a convention under which State B must allow a deduction for the tax levied by State C. State A is obliged to take account only of the net tax paid in State B. This solution is in accordance with the position adopted in conventions already concluded between Member countries. It completely rules out all possibility of a double deduction for the tax levied in the third State in the case where the State of domicile is also obliged to deduct such tax under a convention which it has itself concluded with the third State. However, if the Contracting States consider that the position of the State of domicile should not be affected by the fact that the other State is obliged to deduct the tax levied by a third State, they are free to adopt, by bilateral

agreement, any other solution which is compatible with their respective domestic laws and which rules out the possibility of a double deduction for the tax levied by the third State.

43.   It is not necessary to have a clause maintaining the right of the State of domicile to calculate its tax at a progressive rate. Article 9B implies, in fact, that this State may also, if its domestic law entitles it to do so, tax property falling under Articles 5 and 6 which is situated in the other State. The Convention thus does not lead to any modification in the rate of the tax calculated on the total estate according to the law of the State of domicile.

44.   The State which is not the State of domicile must relinquish its right to tax property, other than that falling under Articles 5 and 6, whether or not such property is taxed in the State of domicile. This applies, in particular, to cases where the State of domicile does not effectively levy tax on the property owing to some particular circumstance as, for example, the operation of a relief, an omission or mistake made by an official, the operation of a statutory time limit. Exceptionally, a derogation could, however, be made in order to maintain the right of the State which is not the State of domicile to impose tax on property other than that falling under Articles 5 and 6, in cases where the law of the State of domicile does not entitle it to tax such other property (see paragraphs 21 *et seq.* above).

45.   The Article contains nothing concerning the application by the State, which is not the State of domicile, of the provisions of its domestic law regarding progressive rates of tax. The Commentary on paragraph 3 of Article 9A in relation to the State of *situs* also applies to Article 9B (see paragraph 38 above).

46.   In order to determine the amount to be allowed as a credit by the State of domicile, it is necessary to convert into that State's currency the amount of tax paid in the other State on the property which that State is entitled to tax under the Convention. The rate of exchange to be used for this conversion is the rate fixed at the time when the tax is paid in that other State.

47.   Each Contracting State is free to determine, according to its domestic law, the vouchers to be produced in proof of the levy and payment of tax in the other State as well as the time limit for the production of the vouchers.

Paragraph 2

Credit to be given for previous gifts

48.   Since taxes on life-time gifts have been included within the scope of the Convention, paragraph 2 provides a rule for the avoidance of double taxation which may arise when one State taxes property which was taxed in the other State on the occasion of a previous gift (see paragraph 17 above).

49.   Under this rule, the State of domicile must give credit for tax paid on property included in its assessment which was the subject of a previous gift and which, at the time of the gift, may have been taxed in the other State in accordance with the provisions of the Convention. It has not, however, to give any credit for tax on previous gifts insofar as that tax has, at the time of the assessment of the gift tax, been already credited by it. This rule is illustrated by the following examples where it is assumed that both Contracting States include previous gifts in the assessment of death duties and that the Convention was applicable on both events. This rule applies not only where the later event is the death of the donor, but also where it is a later gift made by him.

50.   *First case:*   Between the time of the gift and the time of his death the donor remained domiciled in the same State.

EXAMPLE 6   (domicile unchanged)

The donor was at the time of the gift and at the time of his death domiciled in State A. He made a gift to his son of:

Movable property	100
Immovable property situated in State B	200

He died three years later. His sole heir is his son. The estate consists of:

Movable property	700
Immovable property situated in State B	800

The Convention produces the following result (as to the application of progressivity in State B, see paragraph 38 above):

i)   *At the time of the gift:*

State B taxes the immovable property situated in its territory, that is, 200 at 20%	40
State A taxes the whole of the gift, that is, 300 at 15%	45
And has to give credit for State B's tax, but according to paragraph 3 limited to the amount of its own tax on property which may be taxed in State B (see paragraphs 54 *et seq.* below)	– 30
And imposes therefore a net tax	15

That means that 10 of State B's gift tax has not been credited by State A at the time of the gift.

ii)   *At the time of death:*

State B taxes the immovable property forming part of the estate and situated in its territory	800	
It includes that part of the previous gift consisting of immovable property situated in its territory	200	
Basis of assessment	1 000	
It imposes thereon a tax of 50%		500
And giving internal relief for its own previous gift tax[2]		– 40
Net tax on death		460
State A taxes the whole of the estate	1 500	
And it includes within the assessment all previous gifts	300	
Basis of assessment	1 800	
It imposes thereon a tax of 60%		1 080
And gives internal relief for its own previous gift tax[2]		– 45
Tax before credit		1 035

State A has now to give credit for taxes levied in State B:

Under paragraph 1	–460
Under paragraph 2	– 10
Net tax on death	565

2.   See footnote to paragraph 18 above.

The actual tax burden is therefore:

	State A	State B
At the time of the gift	15	40
At the time of death	565	460
	580	500
Total		1 080

51.   *Second case:* Between the time of the gift and the time of his death, the donor changed his domicile from one Contracting State to the other.

EXAMPLE 7   (domicile changed from one Contracting State to the other)

While domiciled in State B the donor made a gift to his son of:

Movable property	100
Immovable property situated in State B	200

Subsequently he changed his domicile to State A and died domiciled there three years later. His sole heir is his son. His estate consists of:

Movable property	700
Immovable property situated in State B	800

The Convention produces the following result (as to the application of progressivity in State B, see paragraph 38 above):

i)   *At the time of the gift:*

State B has the exclusive taxation right on the whole of the gift	300	
And imposes thereon a tax of 20%		60

State A imposes no taxes at all and, at that time, gives no credit for State B's tax.

ii)   *At the time of death:*

State B taxes the immovable property forming part of the estate and situated in its territory	800	
It includes within its assessment that part of the previous gift consisting of immovable property situated in its territory	200	
Basis of assessment	1 000	
It imposes a tax of 50%		500
Giving internal relief for its own tax relating to that part of the previous gift now included within its assessment (that is, 20% of 200)[2]		– 40
Net tax on death		460
State A taxes the whole of the estate	1 500	
And it includes within the assessment all previous gifts	300	
Basis of assessment	1 800	
It imposes thereon a tax of 60%		1 080
And has to give credit for tax levied in State B		
Under paragraph 1		–460
Under paragraph 2		– 60
Net tax		560

2.   See footnote to paragraph 18 above.

The actual tax burden is therefore:

	State A	State B
At the time of the gift	0	60
At the time of death	560	460
	560	520
Total		1 080

52.   The credit to be given by the State of domicile of the deceased under paragraph 2 does not apply to taxes which, on the occasion of the former gift, have been imposed by the other State on property falling under Articles 5 and 6 which is situated in the State of domicile of the deceased. The reason for this limitation is that the country of *situs* should always be entitled to full taxation rights in respect of such property. This limitation is illustrated by the following example:

EXAMPLE 8   (domicile changed from one Contracting State to the other)

While domiciled in State B the donor made a gift to his son of:

Movable property	100
Immovable property situated in State A	200

Subsequently, he changed his domicile to State A and died domiciled there three years later. His sole heir is his son. The estate consists of:

Movable property	700
Immovable property situated in State B	800

Both States use the credit method for the avoidance of double taxation.

The Convention produces the following result (as to the application of progressivity in State B, see paragraph 38 above):

i)   *At the time of the gift:*

State A taxes the immovable property situated in its territory	200	
At 5%		10
State B taxes the whole gift	300	
At 20%		60
And gives credit for State A's tax		– 10
Net tax		50

State B has, therefore, at the time of the gift, imposed a net tax of 30 (20% of 200 = 40 less credit of 10) on the immovable property situated in State A.

ii)   *At the time of death:*

State B taxes the immovable property situated in its territory	800	
At 20%		160
It may not include the previous gift within its assessment.		
State A taxes the whole of the estate	1 500	
And it includes all previous gifts	300	
Basis of assessment	1 800	
It imposes thereon a tax of 60%		1 080
Giving internal relief for its own gift tax[2]		– 10
Tax before credit		1 070

2.   See footnote to paragraph 18 above.

State A has to give credit for State B's taxes

Under paragraph 1	–160
Under paragraph 2 (for the movable property which was part of the gift)	– 20
Net tax	890

The actual tax burden is therefore

	State A	State B
At the time of the gift	10	50
At the time of death	890	160
	900	210
Total		1 110

That is, 30 more than in Examples 6 and 7, because no credit is given by State A for the net gift tax which State B imposed at the time of the gift on the immovable property situated in State A

53.   The observations in paragraphs 34 to 36 above apply, *mutandis mutandis,* also to States using the credit method.

Paragraph 3

"Maximum" deduction

54.   The credit to be given by the State of domicile is equal to the amount of tax paid in the other State on the property which was taxable in that other State. Such credit, however, may not exceed the amount of tax due in the State of domicile in respect of the property taxed in the other State.

55.   The Article implies that if, owing to its domestic law, the State of domicile does not tax certain items or shares of property falling under Articles 5 and 6, for example, agricultural land, the credit is not to be given for tax paid in the State of *situs* to the extent that tax is attributable to such items or shares of property.

56.   Article 9B sets out the main rules of the credit method, but does not give detailed rules on the computation and operation of the credit. This is consistent with the general pattern of the Convention. In many States detailed rules on credit for foreign taxes already exist in their domestic laws. A number of conventions therefore contain a reference to the domestic laws of the Contracting States. However, care should be taken that such domestic rules do not affect the general principle of Article 9B. Where the credit method is not used in the domestic law of a Contracting State, that State should establish rules for the application of Article 9B, if necessary after consultation with the competent authority of the other State.

57.   According to the provision of paragraph 3, the deduction to be allowed in the State of domicile is restricted to that part of its estate, inheritance or gift tax which is appropriate to the property situated in the State of *situs* – the so-called "maximum deduction". Such maximum deduction may be computed either by apportioning the total tax on the estate or gift according to the ratio between the property for which credit is to be given and the total estate or gift, or by applying the rate for the total of the estate or gift to the property for which credit is to be given. In fact, in cases where the tax in the State of *situs* equals or exceeds the appropriate tax in the State of domicile, the credit method will have the same effect as the exemption method with progression. Furthermore, under the credit method, similar problems may arise as regards the amount of property, tax rate etc., as are mentioned in the Commentary on Article 9A

(see especially paragraph 26 above). For the same reason as mentioned in paragraphs 27 and 28 above it is also preferable not to propose an express and uniform solution in the Convention for the credit method but to leave each State free to apply its own legislation and practice. States which prefer to have a special problem solved in their conventions are free to do so in bilateral negotiations.

58.   In calculating the amount of tax due in the State of domicile attributable to the property taxed in the other State, regard must be had to the allocation of the debts of the estate as prescribed in Article 8. This amount must be obtained by applying the average rate of tax levied by the State of domicile to the net value of the property, this being the difference between the value which the State of domicile gives to the property which may be taxed in the other State under Articles 5 and 6 and the amount of the debts to be deducted under Article 8 from that value. In practice, the maximum amount to be deducted (M) is obtained by applying the following formula:

$$M = \text{Amount of tax of State of domicile} \times \frac{\text{Net value of property falling under Article 5 or 6 as included within tax base of State of domicile}}{\text{Total net value of estate}}$$

The following examples illustrate the situation.

59.   *EXAMPLE 9*

The deceased died domiciled in State A. His estate consists of:

Movable property	600	
Immovable property situated in State B	400	
Gross estate	1 000	
A debt which has no economic connection with the immovable property	– 100	
State A imposes tax on	900	
At 20%		180
The immovable property has been taxed in State B on the amount of 400 at 30%		120

State A has to allocate the debt to the movable property, giving a net value of 500. The maximum credit to be given by State A under the Convention is 80, that is, 180 x 400/900. This applies even if the State of domicile would only allow, under its unilateral rules, a deduction of 72 (4/10 of 180) according to the ratio between the gross values of the immovable property situated in State B and of the total estate.

60.   *EXAMPLE 10*

The deceased died domiciled in State A. His estate consists of:

Movable property	600	
Immmovable property situated in State B	400	
Gross estate	1 000	
A debt economically connected with the immovable property (see paragraph 1 of Article 8)	– 100	
State A imposes tax on	900	
At 20%		180

The immovable property has been taxed in State B on an amount of 300 at 30% = 90. State A has to allocate the debt to the immovable property, giving it a net value of 300. In this case the maximum credit to be given by State A under the Convention is 60, that is, 180 × 300/900.

Should, however, the unilateral rules of State A allow a deduction of 72 (see Example 9 above) these more favourable rules of domestic law might have to be applied.

61.   The domestic law of some Member countries contains unilateral measures allowing credit for tax levied in other countries in respect of certain property situated there. When such countries conclude a convention on the lines of this Model, the deduction referred to in Article 9B is intended to supersede such unilateral measures. However, the taxpayers of some States may still be entitled to avail themselves of the unilateral measures provided by the domestic law if they are more advantageous.

62.   The overall effect of the provisions of Article 9B is that the tax calculated by the State of domicile in respect of the total estate or gift is reduced by the smaller of these two amounts:

    a)   that part of the tax calculated by the State of domicile which is attributable to the property, the taxation of which is allowed by the Convention to the other State, or

    b)   the effective amount of tax paid in the other State in respect to such property.

63.   The correct allocation of taxes imposed in the two States to particular items of property eligible for a credit may be important when applying paragraphs 1 and 2. This is illustrated in the following examples:

64.   *EXAMPLE 11*

The deceased died domiciled in State A. His estate consists of:

Movable property	100
Immovable property situated in State B, that is,	
Agricultural land	200
Other immovable property	300
Gross estate	600
State B taxes agricultural land at 15%	30
And the other immovable property at 50%	150
Tax in State B	180
State A taxes the whole estate at 40%	240

In computing the amount of the maximum deduction, two different aproaches are possible:

a)   Under the "item by item" approach the taxes have to be allocated as follows:

Property	State A	State B	Credit due
Movable	40	–	–
Agricultural	80	30	30
Other immovable	120	150	120
Total credit due			150

b) Under the "overall" approach the taxes would have to be allocated as follows:

Property	State A	State B	Credit due
Movable	40	–	–
Immovable	200	180	180
Total credit due			180

Either approach is consistent with the wording of Article 9B. States which want to make clear which approach is to be adopted are free to do so in their bilateral negotiations.

65. **EXAMPLE 12**

The donor, at the time of the gift and at the time of his death, was domiciled in State A. He made a gift to his son of:

Movable property	100
Immovable property situated in State B	200

He died three years later. His sole heir is his son. The estate consists of:

Movable property	700
Immovable property situated in State B	800

The Convention was in force on both occasions. State A uses the credit method.

Both States include previous gifts within their assessments of death duties. They give relief for their own gift tax imposed on the previous gift as follows: State B gives credit for the domestic gift tax actually paid; State A gives credit for the domestic gift tax actually paid, but not less than one half of the estate tax which is attributable to the previous gift.

The Convention produces the following result:

i) *At the time of gift:*

State B taxes the immovable property situated in its territory	200	
At 25%		50
State A taxes the whole of the gift	300	
At 15%		45
And gives credit for State B's tax		– 30
Net tax		15

Thus no credit has been given for 20 of State B's total tax of 50

ii) *At the time of death:*

State B taxes the immovable property forming part of the estate and situated in its territory	800	
It includes from the previous gift the same kind of property	200	
Basis of assessment	1 000	
Tax at 45%		450
Less internal relief for its own gift tax		– 50
Net tax on death		400
State A taxes the whole of the estate	1 500	
And includes all previous gifts	300	
Basis of assessment	1,800	
Tax at 50%		900

Less internal relief for its own gift tax (that is one-half of its own estate tax on the previous gift, 50% x 300) — 75

Tax before credit 825

The credit to be given by State A may be calculated on either of the two approaches referred to in Example 11 (see paragraph 64 above). The different effects of these two approaches are shown in the following tables.

Table A: "Item by Item" approach

Property	Value	Tax		Credit to be given by State A
		In State A	In State B	
Movable (estate)	700	350	0	0
Immovable (estate)	800	400	360	360
Movable (gift)	100	50–25=25	0	0
Immovable (gift)	200	100–50=50	90–50=40	
+ Unrelieved gift tax of State B . .			+20	50
Total		825	420	410

State A has therefore, under this approach, to reduce its tax of	825
By a credit of	410
Leaving a net tax of	415

Table B: "Overall" approach

Property	Value	Tax		Credit to be given by State A
		In State A	In State B	
Movable				
(Estate)	700	350+(50–25)	0	
(Gift)	100	=375		
Immovable				
(Estate)	800	400+(100–50)		
(Gift)	200	=450		
. . . .			360+(90–50)+20 (unrelieved gift tax of State B) = 420	420
Total		825	420	420

State A has therefore, under this approach, to reduce its tax of	825
For the full amount of State B's taxes by a credit of	420
Leaving a net tax of	405

66. The limitations contained in Article 9B may, in very rare and special cases, lead to unrelieved double taxation so far as previous gifts are concerned. The following example illustrates this:

EXAMPLE 13

The donor, at the time of the gift and at the time of his death, was domiciled in State A.

He made a gift to his son of immovable property situated in State B	200	
He died three years later. His sole heir is his son. The estate consists of:		
Movable property	500	
Immovable property situated in State B	300	

The Convention was applicable on both occasions. Both States include previous gifts within their assessments of death duties. State A uses the credit method. The Convention will produce the following result:

i) *At the time of gift:*

State B taxes the immovable property situated in its territory	200	
At 10%		20
State A taxes that immovable property	200	
At 35%		70
Giving credit for State B's tax		− 20
Net tax		50

ii) *At the time of death:*

State B taxes the immovable property forming part of the estate	300	
And includes the previous gift	200	
Basis of assessment	500	
Tax at 50%		250
Less internal relief for its own gift tax[2]		− 20
Net tax on death		230
State A taxes the whole of the estate	800	
And includes the previous gift	200	
Basis of assessment	1 000	
Tax at 40%		400
Less internal relief for its own gift tax[2]		− 70
Tax before credit		330

The taxes imposed in the two States are as follows:

---

2. See footnote to paragraph 18 above.

Property	Value	Tax		Credit to be given by State A
		In State A	In State B	
Movable	500	200	0	0
Immovable (estates)	300	120	150	120
Immovable (gift)	200	10	80	10
Total		330	230	130
State A has therefore, to reduce its tax of				330
By a credit of				130
Leaving a net tax of				200

At the time of death, the part of State B's tax which is attributable to the previous gift is 80. The credit against State A's death duties is only 10, although, at the time when the gift was made, State A levied a tax on the gift exceeding that of State B by 50 [see *i)* above]. The same result will occur if State A, under its domestic law, does not include that previous gift at the time of death.

67.   Unrelieved double taxation similar to that detailed in Example 13 above may also arise in cases where the State of domicile taxes a gift only at the time when it was made, whereas the State of *situs* only taxes the gift as part of the deceased's estate.

68.   These cases of double taxation could be avoided in various ways:
   a)   the State of domicile could re-open its assessment of gift tax and give credit for the later estate tax of the State of *situs* to the extent that credit has not previously been given (or make a corresponding refund); or
   b)   the State of *situs* could give credit for the previous gift tax of the State of domicile.

69.   The Committee on Fiscal Affairs considered that the inclusion of provisions giving effect to these solutions would lead to an unnecessary complication of the Convention, especially as these cases will rarely occur in practice. States are, however, free to provide their own solutions in their bilateral negotiations.

IV.   SPECIAL PROBLEMS CONCERNING ARTICLES 9A AND 9B

A.   Subsidiary taxation for various reasons by the State which is not the State of the deceased's or the donor's domicile

70.   It may happen that the State which is not the State of the deceased's or the donor's domicile within the meaning of the Convention could, under its domestic law, impose a comprehensive tax liability for one or more of the reasons given in paragraph 5 of the Commentary on Article 1. This State may want to keep at least a subsidiary taxation right on the property falling under Article 7 (see also paragraphs 5 to 7 of the Commentary on Article 7).

71.   In principle, Member countries should adhere to the rules provided by the Convention. There may, however, be a compelling reason to deviate from these rules in the cases mentioned in paragraph 70 above especially where the deceased, in contemplation of death, or the donor, in contemplation of making a gift, has moved his domicile to the other State with the intention of escaping taxation by his former State of domicile. Where States retain a subsidiary right to impose tax for any of the reasons given in paragraph 5 of the Commentary on Article 1, that right should be retained for a limited period only, and in any event, not longer than ten years after the deceased or the donor has ceased to be domiciled in their territory. Moreover, other restrictions may be imposed on a subsidiary taxation right retained by the State of former domicile.

72.   In their bilateral conventions States which want to retain a subsidiary comprehensive taxation right on the grounds of nationality of the deceased or donor are free to add to Articles 9A or 9B a further paragraph on the lines of the draft model provisions outlined below. These models may be modified to meet other special criteria (for example, secondary domicile of the deceased or the donor, domicile or nationality of the heir, legatee or donee).

73.   *Model Provisions*

a)   *Exemption method*

"4.   However, where the deceased or the donor had been domiciled in the other Contracting State at any time within the ten years preceding the date of his death or, as the case may be, the time when the gift was made, and he is a national of that other Contracting State, that other Contracting State also may tax property falling under Article 7 in accordance with its domestic law, but it shall relieve double taxation on such property in the following way:

    a)   it shall exempt, by applying paragraphs 1 to 3 of this Article, as if it were the State of domicile of the deceased or the donor, immovable property situated in the former Contracting State and movable property of permanent establishments or fixed bases as referred to in paragraphs 1 and 6 of Article 6, which are situated in the former Contracting State;

    b)   in respect of other property, it shall allow as a deduction from the tax calculated according to its domestic law an amount equal to the tax paid in the former Contracting State on such property in relation to the same event and on a previous gift in accordance with the provisions of the Convention, to the extent that such a deduction has not been allowed at the time of that gift. The deduction shall not, however, exceed that part of the tax of that other Contracting State, as computed before any deduction is made, which is attributable to such property."

b)   *Credit Method*

"4.   However, where the deceasd or the donor had been domiciled in the other Contracting State at any time within the ten years preceding the date of his death or, as the case may be, the time when the gift was made, and he is a national of that other Contracting State, that other Contracting State also may tax property falling under Article 7, in accordance with its domestic law, but it shall allow as a deduction from such tax an amount equal to the tax which has been paid in the former Contracting State on such property by applying the provisions of paragraphs 1 to 3 as if it were the State of domicile of the deceased or the donor."

74.   The following example illustrates these model provisions:

EXAMPLE 14

The deceased, who was a national of State B and had been domiciled there within ten years of his death, died domiciled in State A. His sole heir is his son. His estate consists of:

Immovable property situated in State A	700
Immovable property situated in State B	800
Immovable property situated in a third State	900
Movable property	500
Total	2 900

There exists a double taxation convention between States A and B, the relevant Article 9 of which includes the addition mentioned in paragraph 73 above.

Under domestic law, both States may tax the total of the estate. The rate of tax is 50% in State A and 60% in State B.

Taxation in State A:

If State A applies the exemption method, it will exempt the immovable property situated in State B (800) and tax the remaining estate (2 100) at 50%	1 050
If State uses the credit method, it will tax the total of the estate (2 900) at 50%	1 450
And give credit for State B's tax on the immovable property situated in State B up to the amount of its own tax attributable to that property that is, 50% of 800	– 400
Net tax	1 050

Taxation in State B:

Without the model provision, State B could always tax only the immovable property situated in its territory, that is, 800. By including the model provision the situation changes as follows:

If State B applies the exemption method it will exempt, under subparagraph a) of the model provision A, the immovable property situated in State A (700) and tax the remaining estate of 2 200 at 60%	1 320
State B has then, under subparagraph b) of the Model provision A, to give credit for State A's tax on the remaining items falling under Article 7, that is, on the immovable property situated in the third State (900) and the movable property (500) making a total of 50% of 1 400	700
Net tax	620
If State B uses the credit method it will tax the total estate of 2 900 at 60%	1 740
And, under the model provision B, will give credit for State A's tax on the property falling under Article 7 that is, 50% of 2 100 (700 + 900 + 500)	–1 050
Net tax	690

B. Time limits for the application of paragraph 2 of Articles 9A and 9B

75.   The Committee on Fiscal Affairs considered whether a time limit should be set for the application of paragraph 2 of Articles 9A and 9B in the sense that the paragraph would only apply where the time between the previous gift and the death or later gift did not exceed a specified limit period. The adoption of such a time limit can be justified by two main reasons:

    a)   the two Contracting States may intend to cover only near-death gifts by the application of paragraph 2 of Articles 9A or 9B. In such a case the time limit would have to be a relatively short one;

    b)   some Member countries, when imposing death duties or gift taxes, take into account previous gifts made within a certain time before the death or later gift, but the period varies considerably from country to country. States may consider that a time limit would remove administrative difficulties caused by retaining details of gift tax assessments longer than is required for their own tax purposes. Then, however, such a time limit would be necessary only where the domestic laws of the two Contracting States differ and it should be near the shorter of the two periods.

76.   Such a time limit could operate in two ways:

    a)   by restricting the right of the Contracting States to include previous gifts within later assessments if they were made more than a certain period of time before death or a later gift; or

    b)   by restricting the application of paragraph 2 of Articles 9A or 9B to gifts which were made within a certain time before death or a later gift.

77.   The Committee on Fiscal Affairs decided not to suggest such time limits for the following reasons:

    a)   the principle laid down in subparagraph *a)* of paragraph 76 above would restrict the taxation rights of Member countries in a way which is not usual in double taxation conventions;

    b)   the principle laid down in subparagraph *b)* of paragraph 76 would favour near-death gifts which are more likely to have been made with the intention of avoiding or reducing later death duties than gifts made much earlier, and therefore such a provision should be introduced only where the difficulties mentioned in subparagraph *b)* of paragraph 75 above become compelling.

C. Application of the credit method between States with different forms of death duties

78.   The application of the credit method may become difficult between Contracting States where one of them imposes an estate tax, that is, it taxes the estate as a whole, whereas the other State imposes an inheritance tax, that is, it imposes tax on such parts of the estate as devolved on different heirs or legatees. The following example illustrates some of the difficulties which may arise:

79. **EXAMPLE 15**

The deceased died domiciled in State A. His estate consists of three items of immovable property situated in State B, the values of which are:

Building 1	300
Building 2	600
Building 3	900
And movable property valued at	1 200
Total	3 000

Under his will the estate goes equally to his wife, his son and his mother. The 1,000 share of each beneficiary may be taken in numerous ways. The rates of tax in the State which levies the inheritance tax are 5% for the wife, 10% for the son and 15% for the mother. The State which levies the estate tax gives a partial exemption of 70 for property going to the wife, of 30 for property going to the son and taxes the remaining estate at a flat rate of 10%.

80. If the State of domicile is the one which levies the estate tax, it may have to decide to what extent it has to give credit against its uniformly levied tax for the taxes which have been levied in the State of *situs* on different persons at different rates. *Vice versa*, if the State of domicile levies the inheritance tax, it may have to decide which taxes levied in a lump sum on the estate in the State of *situs* have to be attributed to the different heirs who have taken possession of the different parts of the estate. Member countries are free to settle these difficulties in bilateral negotiations.

RESERVATION ON THE ARTICLE

81. As *New Zealand* has no provision for credit for duty on gifts the Article has no application in New Zealand in relation to gifts.

COMMENTARY ON ARTICLE 10
CONCERNING NON-DISCRIMINATION

I. PRELIMINARY REMARKS

1.   Provisions against discrimination on grounds of nationality already appear, for all taxes, in Article 24 of the 1977 Income Tax Model. From the outset, it is necessary to emphasize that, notwithstanding the provisions of Article 2 which determines the taxes on estates and inheritances and on gifts covered by the Convention, the non-discrimination provisions in Article 10 concern taxes of every kind and description.

2.   The incorporation of a provision barring discrimination on grounds of national-ity, in a Convention which has the limited object of avoiding double taxation with respect to taxes on estates and inheritances and on gifts, may seem superfluous when a convention which excludes such discrimination in relation to all taxes already exists between two Contracting States. This incorporation may, however, be of some value if the latter convention is terminated or for other reasons. Therefore it has been found appropriate to include a non-discrimination Article in this Convention. It was decided not to include paragraphs 4 to 6 of Article 24 of the 1977 Income Tax Model since the provisions of those paragraphs relate, more or less exclusively, to taxes on income and capital and are not appropriate in the concept of this Model. Contracting States are, however, free to include the whole of Article 24 of the 1977 Income Tax Model within their conventions dealing with death duties and gift taxes.

II. COMMENTARY ON THE PROVISION OF THE ARTICLE

Paragraph 1

3.   This paragraph establishes the principle that, for the purposes of taxation, discrimination on the grounds of nationality is forbidden, and that, subject to reciprocity, the nationals of one Contracting State may not be less favourably treated in the other Contracting State than nationals of the latter State in the same circumstances. In the case of taxes on estates, inheritances and gifts, this principle must be applied with regard to the deceased or to the donor, and to the heirs and legatees or to the donees. Thus, one Contracting State may not subject the estates of, or gifts made by, nationals of the other State in the same circumstances to taxation which is more burdensome than that applying to estates of, or gifts made by, its own nationals. Similarly, heirs, legatees or donees who are nationals of one State may not be treated less favourably in the other State than nationals of the latter State in the same circumstances.

4.   The expression "in the same circumstances" which appears in the text refers to taxpayers (individuals, legal persons, partnerships and associations) placed, from the point of view of the application of the ordinary taxation law and regulations, in substantially similar circumstances both in law and in fact. In relation to taxes on estates, inheritances and on gifts, the expression equally applies to the deceased and the donor as well as to the heirs, legatees and donees.

5.   Consequently, if one of the Contracting States, in giving relief from taxation on account of family responsibilities, distinguishes between its own nationals according to whether they reside in its territory or not, that State cannot be obliged to give nationals of the other State, who do not reside in its territory, the same treatment as it gives its resident nationals but it undertakes to extend to them the same treatment as is available to its non-resident nationals.

6.   Likewise, the provisions of paragraph 1 are not to be construed as obliging a State, which accords special taxation privileges to its own public bodies or services, to extend the same privileges to the public bodies and services of the other State.

7.   Neither are they to be construed as obliging a State which accords special taxation privileges to private non-profit-making institutions whose activities are performed for purposes of public benefit which are specific to that State, to extend the same privileges to similar institutions of the other State.

8.   To take the first of these two cases, if a State accords immunity from taxation to its own public bodies and services, this is justified because such bodies and services are integral parts of that State and at no time can their circumstances be comparable to those of the public bodies and services of the other State. Nevertheless, this reservation is not intended to apply to State corporations carrying on gainful undertakings. To the extent that these can be regarded as being on the same footing as private industrial and commercial undertakings, the provisions of paragraph 1 will apply to them.

9.   As for the second case, if a State accords taxation privileges to certain private non-profit-making institutions, this is clearly justified by the very nature of these institutions' activities and by the benefit which that State and its nationals will derive from those activities.

10.   The Contracting States are free to adopt another proposition in this matter especially with regard to taxes on estates, inheritances and on gifts. Circumstances may prompt them to treat such public bodies and private institutions of both countries in the same way. Similarity of treatment can be effected by the text proposed below:

> "1.   Exemptions from, and reductions of tax accorded by, the law of a Contracting State to that State or to its political subdivisions or local authorities shall apply to the other Contracting State and to the political subdivisions and local authorities of that other State".
> "2.   Organisations of a Contracting State shall be entitled in the other Contracting State to any exemptions from, or reductions of tax accorded to, organisations of the same type of that other State. The type of the organisations shall be determined according to the domestic law of the State imposing the tax."

11.   Furthermore, paragraph 1 has been deliberately framed in a negative form. By providing that the nationals of one State may not be subjected in the other State to any

taxation or any requirement connected therewith which is other, or more burdensome than, the taxation and connected requirements to which nationals of the other Contracting State in the same circumstances are, or may be, subjected, this paragraph has the same mandatory force as if it enjoined the Contracting States to accord the same treatment to their nationals. However, since the principal object of this clause is to forbid discrimination in one State against the nationals of the other, there is nothing to prevent the former State from granting to persons of foreign nationality, for special reasons of its own, or in order to comply with a special stipulation in a double taxation convention, certain concessions or facilities which are not available to its own nationals. As worded, paragraph 1 would not prohibit this.

12.   Subject to the foregoing observations, the words "... shall not be subject ... to any taxation or any requirement connected therewith which is other or more burdensome ..." mean that when tax is imposed on nationals and foreigners in the same circumstances, it must be in the same form for both, its basis of charge and method of assessment must be the same, its rate must be the same, and, finally, the formalities connected with the taxation (returns, payment, prescribed times, etc.) must not be more onerous for foreigners than for nationals.

Paragraph 2

13.   This paragraph merely stipulates that the term "nationals" applies to all individuals possessing the nationality of one of the Contracting States. It has not been judged necessary here to introduce into the text of the Article any considerations relating to the meaning given to the concept of nationality, any more than it seemed indispensable to make any special comment here on the meaning and application of the word. Obviously, in determining in relation to individuals what is meant by "the nationals of a Contracting State", reference must be made to the sense in which the term is usually employed and to each State's particular rules on the acquisition or loss of nationality.

14.   However, paragraph 2 is more specific as to legal persons, partnerships and associations. By declaring that all legal persons, partnerships and associations deriving their status as such from the law in force in a Contracting State are considered to be nationals for the purposes of paragraph 1 the provision disposes of a difficulty which often arises in determining the nationality of companies. In defining the nationality of companies, certain States have regard less to the law which governs the company than to the origin of the capital with which the company was formed or the nationality of the individuals or legal persons controlling it. No ambiguity need be apprehended therefore.

15.   Moreover, in view of the legal relationship created between the company and the State under whose law it is constituted, which from certain points of view is closely akin to the relationship of nationality in the case of individuals, it seems justifiable not to deal with legal persons, partnerships and associations in a special provision, but to bring them within the same expression as individuals.

Paragraph 3

16.   On 28th September, 1954, a number of States concluded in New York a Convention relating to the status of stateless persons, under Article 29 of which stateless persons must be accorded national treatment. The signatories of the Convention include several OECD Member countries.

17.   It should, however, be recognised that the provisions of paragraph 3 will, in a bilateral convention, enable national treatment to be extended to stateless persons who, because they are in one of the situations enumerated in paragraph 2 of Article 1 of the above-mentioned Convention of 28th September, 1954, are not covered by that Convention. This is mainly the case, on the one hand, of persons receiving at the time of the signature of that Convention, protection or assistance from organs or agencies of the United Nations other than the United Nations High Commissioner for Refugees, and, on the other hand, of persons who are residents of a country and who there enjoy and are subject to the rights and obligations attaching to the possession of that country's nationality.

18.   The purpose of paragraph 3 is to limit the scope of the clause concerning equality of treatment with nationals of a Contracting State solely to stateless persons who are domiciled in that or the other Contracting State.

19.   By thus excluding stateless persons who are domiciled in neither Contracting State, such a clause prevents their being privileged in one State as compared with nationals of the other State.

20.   However, if Contracting States consider it desirable, in their bilateral negotiations, to extend the application of paragraph 3 to all stateless persons, whether domiciled in a Contracting State or not, so that in all cases they would enjoy the most favourable treatment accorded to nationals of the Contracting State concerned, they need only to adopt the following text which contains no condition as to domicile in a Contracting State:

> "Notwithstanding the provisions of Article 1, stateless persons shall not be subjected in a Contracting State to any taxation or any requirement connected therewith which is other or more burdensome than the taxation and connected requirements to which nationals of that State in the same circumstances are or may be subjected".

21.   It is possible that in the future certain States will take exception to the provisions of paragraph 3 as being too liberal insofar as they entitle stateless persons who are domiciled in one State to claim equality of treatment, not only in the other State, but also in their State of domicile and thus benefit in particular in the latter from the provisions of double taxation conventions concluded by it with third States with which they may have absolutely no personal or economic link. If such States wished to avoid this latter consequence, they would have to modify paragraph 3 as follows:

> "Stateless persons who are domiciled in a Contracting State shall not be subjected in the other Contracting State to any taxation, or any requirement connected therewith, which is other or more burdensome than the taxation and connected requirements to which nationals of that other State in the same circumstances are or may be subjected".

22.   Finally, it should be understood that the definition of the term "stateless person" to be used for the purposes of such a clause can only be that laid down in paragraph 1 of Article 1 of the Convention of 28th September, 1954, which defines a stateless person as "a person who is not considered as a national by any State under the operation of its law".

Paragraph 4

23.   This paragraph states that the scope of the Article is not restricted by the provisions of Article 2. The Article therefore applies to taxes of every kind and description levied by, or on behalf of, the State, its political subdivisions or local authorities. On the other hand, some Member countries, in their conventions covering taxes on estates and inheritances and on gifts, restrict the operation of this Article to the taxes covered by the Convention. States are free to do so in their bilateral negotiations.

RESERVATION ON THE ARTICLE

24.   Since the *United States* imposes tax on the total estates of all citizens irrespective of domicile at the time of death, it reserves the right to grant exemptions, deductions and other benefits to the estates of United States citizens domiciled abroad which are not granted to the estates of non-nationals not domiciled in the United States.

COMMENTARY ON ARTICLE 11
CONCERNING MUTUAL AGREEMENT PROCEDURE

I. PRELIMINARY REMARKS

1. This Article institutes a mutual agreement procedure for resolving difficulties arising out of the application of the Convention in the broadest sense of the term.

2. It provides firstly, in paragraphs 1 and 2, that the competent authorities shall endeavour by mutual agreement to resolve the situation of taxpayers subjected to taxation not in accordance with the provisions of the Convention.

3. It also, in paragraph 3, invites and authorises the competent authorities of the two Contracting States to resolve by mutual agreement problems relating to the interpretation or application of the Convention and, furthermore, to consult together for the elimination of double taxation in cases not provided for in the Convention.

4. Finally, as regards the practical operation of the mutual agreement procedure, the Article, in paragraph 4, authorises the competent authorities to communicate with each other directly, without going through diplomatic channels, and, if it seems advisable to them, to have an oral exchange of opinions through a Joint Commission appointed especially for the purpose.

5. Since the Article merely lays down general rules concerning the mutual agreement procedure, the comments now following are intended to clarify the purpose of such rules, and also to amplify them, if necessary, by referring, in particular, to the rules followed at international level in the conduct of mutual agreement procedures or at the internal level in the conduct of the procedures which exist in most Member countries for dealing with disputed claims regarding taxes.

II. COMMENTARY ON THE PROVISIONS OF THE ARTICLE

Paragraphs 1 and 2

6. The rules laid down in paragraphs 1 and 2 provide for the elimination in a particular case of taxation which does not accord with the Convention. As is known in such cases it is normally open to taxpayers to litigate in the tax court, either immediately or upon the dismissal of their objections by the taxation authorities. When taxation not in accordance with the Convention arises from an incorrect application of the Convention in both States, taxpayers are then obliged to litigate in each State, with all the disadvantages and uncertainties that such a situation entails. Therefore, paragraph 1 makes a special procedure available to taxpayers affected, without depriving them of the ordinary legal remedies available. The first stage of this procedure is

conducted exclusively in the State to which the taxpayer has appealed and lasts from the presentation of the objection up to the decision by the competent authority of that State. In its second stage the procedure is aimed at resolving the dispute on an amicable basis, that is, by agreement between competent authorities, and therefore it is called the mutual agreement procedure. Paragraph 1 entitles heirs or legatees and all other persons legally appointed to realise or administer the deceased person's estate ("exécuteur testamentaire", administrators, executors or trustees in legal systems of the Anglo-American type, etc.), and the donor or donee, to apply to the competent authority of either State.

7.   In any case, the mutual agreement procedure is clearly a special procedure outside the domestic law. It follows that it can be set in motion solely in cases coming within paragraph 1, that is, cases where tax has been charged, or is going to be charged, contrary to the provisions of the Convention. Thus, where a charge of tax has been made contrary both to the Convention and the domestic law, this case is amenable to the mutual agreement procedure only to the extent that the Convention is affected, unless a connecting link exists between the rules of the Convention and the rules of the domestic law which have been misapplied.

8.   In practice, the procedure applies to cases, likely to be the most numerous, where the tax charges in question lead to double taxation which it is the specific purpose of the Convention to avoid. Among the most common cases, mention must be made of the following:

- differences of interpretation by the two Contracting States as to the determination of domicile (paragraph 2 of Article 4) or the existence of a permanent establishment or a fixed base (Article 6);
- questions relating to the allocation of debts (Article 8);
- conflicts between the domestic laws of the Contracting States as to whether property falls under Articles 5 and 6 or Article 7.

9.   The mutual agreement procedure is also applicable in the absence of any double taxation contrary to the Convention, once the taxation in dispute is in direct contravention of a rule in the Convention. Such is the case when one State taxes a particular class of property in respect of which the Convention gives the exclusive right to tax to the other State even though the latter is unable under its domestic law to exercise that right. Another category of cases concerns persons who, being nationals of one Contracting State but domiciled in the other State, are subjected in that other State to taxation treatment which is discriminatory under the provisions of Article 10.

10.   It should be noted that the mutual agreement procedure, unlike the disputed claims procedure under domestic law, can be set in motion by a taxpayer without waiting until the taxation considered by him to be "not in accordance with the Convention" has been charged against or notified to him. To be able to set the procedure in motion, he needs only to establish that the "actions of one or both of the Contracting States" will result in such taxation.

11.   To be admissible, objections presented under paragraph 1 must first meet the twofold requirement expressly formulated in that paragraph: they must be presented to the competent authority of one of the Contracting States, and they must be so presented within three years of the first notification of the action which gives rise to taxation which is not in accordance with the Convention.

119

12.   As to the first of those requirements, Article 11 differs from the provisions of Article 25 of the 1977 Income Tax Model under which the taxpayer has normally to present his case to the State of which he is a resident, that is, to the State with which he is more closely connected. In contrast, in the case of death duties, the "State of domicile" is that with which the *deceased* was more closely connected. There is no reason to oblige the actual taxpayer to present his case to the competent authority of the State of domicile of the deceased if the taxpayer is personally more closely connected with the other Contracting State. The Committee on Fiscal Affairs decided therefore to leave the taxpayer the choice of addressing himself to either of the Contracting States and did not consider it necessary to provide a different solution for gift taxes.

13.   The time limit of three years for presenting objections is intended to protect administrations from late objections. This time limit must be regarded as a minimum, so that Contracting States are left free to agree in their bilateral negotiations upon a longer period in the interest of taxpayers, for example, by analogy with the time limits laid down by their respective domestic regulations in regard to tax objections. Contracting States may omit the second sentence of paragraph 1 if they agree that their respective domestic regulations apply automatically to such objections and are more favourable to the taxpayers affected either because they allow a longer time for presenting objections or because they do not set any time limits for such purpose.

14.   The provision fixing the starting point of the three-year time limit as the date of the "first notification of the action resulting in taxation not in accordance with the provisions of the Convention" should be interpreted in the way most favourable to the taxpayer. Thus, even if such taxation should be directly charged in pursuance of an administrative decision or action of general application, the time limit begins to run only from the date of the notification of the individual action giving rise to such taxation, that is to say, under the most favourable interpretation, from the act of taxation itself, as evidenced by a notice of assessment or an official demand or other instrument for the collection or levy of tax. Furthermore, where it is the combination of decisions or actions taken in both States resulting in taxation not in accordance with the Convention, it begins to run only from the first notification of the most recent decision or action.

15.   The Convention does not lay down any special rules as to the form of the objection. The competent authorities may prescribe such special rules. If no special rules have been made, the objections may be presented in the same form as objections regarding taxes are presented to the tax authorities of the State concerned.

16.   As regards the procedure itself, it is necessary to consider the two distinct stages into which it is divided (see paragraph 6 above).

17.   In the first stage, which opens with the presentation of the taxpayer's objections, the procedure takes place exclusively at the level of dealings between him and the competent authority of the State to which he has applied. Paragraph 1 gives the taxpayer concerned the right to apply to any one of the competent authorities of a Contracting State, whether or not he has exhausted all the remedies available to him under the domestic law of each of the two States. On the other hand, the competent authority to which he applies is under an obligation to consider whether the objection is justified and, if it appears to be justified, to take action on it in one of the two forms provided for in paragraph 2.

18.   If the competent authority duly approached recognises that the complaint is justified and considers that the taxation complained of is due wholly or in part to a

measure taken in that State, it must give the complainant satisfaction as speedily as possible by making such adjustments or allowing such reliefs as appear to be justified. In this situation, the issue can be resolved without resort to the mutual agreement procedure. On the other hand, it may be found useful to exchange views and information with the competent authority of the other State in order, for example, to confirm a given interpretation of the convention.

19.   If, however, it appears to that competent authority that the taxation complained of is due wholly or in part to a measure taken in the other State, it will be incumbent on it, indeed it will be its duty, as clearly appears by the terms of paragraph 2, to set in motion the mutual agreement procedure proper.

20.   A taxpayer is entitled to present his case under paragraph 1 to the competent authority of either State, whether or not he may also have made a claim or commenced litigation under the domestic laws of those States. If litigation is pending the competent authority of the State applied to should not wait for the final adjudication, but should say whether it considers the case to be eligible for the mutual agreement procedure. If it so decides, it has to determine whether it is itself able to arrive at a satisfactory solution or whether the case has to be submitted to the competent authority of the other State.

21.   If a claim has been finally adjudicated by a court in the State to which the taxpayer has applied, the taxpayer may still wish to present or pursue a claim under the mutual agreement procedure. In some States, the competent authority may be able to arrive at a satisfactory solution which departs from the court decision. In other States, the competent authority may be bound by the court decision. It may nevertheless present the case to the competent authority of the other Contracting State and ask the latter to take measures for avoiding taxation which is contrary to the convention.

22.   In its second stage, which opens with the approach to the competent authority of the other State by the competent authority to which the taxpayer has applied, the procedure is thenceforward at the level of dealings between States, as if the State to which the complaint was presented had given it its backing. While this procedure is indisputably a procedure between States, it may nevertheless be asked:

–   whether, as the title of the Article and the terms employed in the first sentence of paragraph 2 suggest, it is no more than a simple procedure of mutual agreement, or constitutes the implementation of a *"pactum de contrahendo"* laying on the parties a duty merely to negotiate but in no way laying on them a duty to reach agreement; or
–   whether, on the contrary, it is to be regarded (on the assumption of course that it takes place within the framework of a Joint Commission) as a procedure of a jurisdictional nature laying on the parties a duty to resolve the dispute.

23.   Paragraph 2 no doubt entails a duty to negotiate; but as far as reaching mutual agreement through the procedure is concerned, the competent authorities are merely under a duty to use their best endeavours. However, Contracting States could agree on a more far-reaching commitment whereby the mutual agreement procedure, and above all the discussions in the Joint Commission, would produce a solution to the dispute. Such a rule could be established either by an amendment to paragraph 2 or by an interpretation specified in a protocol or an exchange of letters annexed to the convention.

24.   In seeking a mutual agreement, the competent authorities must first determine their position in the light of the rules of their respective taxation laws and of the provisions of the Convention, which are as binding on them as they are on the taxpayer. Should the strict application of such rules or provisions preclude any agreement, it may reasonably be held that the competent authorities, as in the case of international arbitration, can, subsidiarily, have regard to considerations of equity in order to give the taxpayer satisfaction.

25.   The purpose of the last sentence of paragraph 2 is to enable countries with time limits relating to adjustments of assessments and tax refunds in their domestic laws to give effect to an agreement despite such time limits. It also prevents a State from using the time limits laid down in its domestic law to negate the mutual agreement entered into with the other State. Some States, however, may be unable, on constitutional or other legal grounds, to enter into a mutual agreement procedure which overrides the time limits laid down in their domestic laws. Other States may be able to override their domestic laws but may wish for other reasons, for example, administrative reasons, to insert a specific time limit in the second sentence of paragraph 2. In such cases that sentence should be deleted or amended.

26.   Apart from time limits, there may exist other obstacles such as "final court decisions" to giving effect to an agreement. States are free to agree on firm provisions for the removal of such obstacles.

27.   Finally, the case may arise where a mutual agreement is concluded in relation to a taxpayer who has brought a suit for the same purpose in the competent court of either State and which is still pending. In such a case, there would be no grounds for rejecting a request by a taxpayer that he be allowed to defer acceptance of the solution agreed upon as a result of the mutual agreement procedure until the court had delivered its judgment in the suit still pending. On the other hand, it is necessary to take into account the concern of the competent authority to avoid any divergence or contradiction between the decision of the court and the mutual agreement, with the difficulties or risks of abuse that they could entail. In short, therefore, it seems reasonable that the implementation of a mutual agreement should be made subject:

– to the acceptance of such mutual agreement by the taxpayer, and
– to the taxpayer's withdrawal of his suit at law concerning the points settled in the mutual agreement.

Paragraph 3

28.   The first sentence of this paragraph invites and authorises the competent authorities to resolve, if possible, difficulties of interpretation or application by means of mutual agreement. These are essentially difficulties of a general nature which concern, or which may concern, a category of taxpayers, even if they have arisen in connection with an individual case normally coming under the procedure defined in paragraphs 1 and 2.

29.   This provision makes it possible to resolve difficulties arising from the application of the convention. Such difficulties are not only those of a practical nature, which might arise in connection with the setting up and operation of procedures for the relief from tax in a Contracting State, but also those which could impair or impede the normal operation of the provisions of the convention as they were conceived by the

negotiators, the solution of which does not depend on a prior agreement as to the interpretation of the convention.

30.   Under this provision the competent authorities can, in particular:

- where a term has been incompletely or ambiguously defined in the convention, complete or clarify its definition in order to obviate any difficulty;
- where the laws of a Contracting State have been changed without impairing the balance or affecting the substance of the convention, settle any difficulties that may emerge from the new system of taxation arising out of such changes.

31.   Paragraph 3 confers on the "competent authorities of the Contracting States", as defined in paragraph 1 of Article 3, that is, generally the Ministers of Finance or their authorised representatives normally responsible for the administration of the convention, authority to resolve by mutual agreement any difficulties arising as to the interpretation of the convention. However, it is important not to lose sight of the fact that, depending on the domestic laws of Contracting States, other authorities (Ministry of Foreign Affairs, courts) have the right to interpret international treaties and agreements as well as the "competent authority" designated in the Convention, and that this is sometimes the exclusive right of such other authorities.

32.   Mutual agreements resolving general difficulties of interpretation or application are binding on administrations as long as the competent authorities do not agree to modify or rescind the mutual agreement.

33.   The second sentence of paragraph 3 enables the competent authorities to deal also with such cases of double taxation as do not come within the scope of the provisions of the convention. If is of course desirable that the mutual agreement procedure should result in the effective elimination of the double taxation which can occur in such a situation. An exception must, however, be made for the case of Contracting States whose domestic laws prevent the convention from being made applicable by the mutual agreement procedure to points which are not explicitly or at least implicitly dealt with; in that case, the convention could be supplemented only by a protocol subject, like the convention itself, to ratification or approval.

Paragraph 4

34.   This paragraph determines how the competent authorities may consult together for the resolution by mutual agreement, either of an individual case coming under the procedure defined in paragraphs 1 and 2, or of general problems relating in particular to the interpretation or application of the convention, and which are referred to in paragraph 3.

35.   It provides firstly that the competent authorities may communicate with each other directly. It would therefore not be necessary to go through diplomatic channels.

36.   Such exchange of opinions will normally take place by letter. However, if the competent authorities deem it useful, in order to reach an agreement more easily, they may also, as provided in the second sentence of paragraph 4, exchange views orally. They may, moreover, agree that such exchanges should take place in a commission consisting of representatives of the said authorities.

37.   As to this Joint Commission, paragraph 4 leaves it to the competent authorities of the Contracting States to determine the number of members and the rules of procedure of this body.

38.   However, while the Contracting States may avoid any formalism in this field, it is nevertheless their duty to give taxpayers whose cases are brought before the Joint Commission under paragraph 2 certain essential guarantees, namely:

- the right to make representations in writing or orally, either in person or through a representative;
- the right to be assisted by counsel.

39.   However, disclosure to the taxpayer or his representatives of the papers in the case does not seem to be warranted, in view of the special nature of the procedure.

40.   Without infringing upon the freedom of choice enjoyed in principle by the competent authorities in designating their representatives on the Joint Commission, it would be desirable for them to agree to entrust the chairmanship of each delegation, which might include one or more representatives of the service responsible for the procedure, to a high official or judge chosen primarily on account of his special experience; it is reasonable to believe, in fact, that the participation of such persons would be likely to facilitate reaching an agreement.

III.   FINAL OBSERVATIONS

41.   On the whole, the mutual agreement procedure appearing in existing conventions and similar to that recommended here has proved satisfactory. The most recent treaty practice shows that Article 11 represents the maximum that Contracting States are prepared to accept. It must, however, be admitted that this provision is not yet entirely satisfactory from the taxpayer's viewpoint. This is because the competent authorities are required only to seek a solution and are not obliged to find one (see paragraph 23 above). The conclusion of a mutual agreement depends to a large extent on the powers of compromise which the domestic laws allow the competent authorities. Thus, if a convention is interpreted or applied differently in two Contracting States, and if the competent authorities are unable to agree on a joint solution whithin the framework of a mutual agreement procedure, double taxation is still possible although contrary to the sense and purpose of a convention aimed at avoiding double taxation.

42.   It is difficult to avoid this situation without going outside the framework of the mutual agreement procedure. The first approach to a solution might consist of seeking an advisory opinion: the two Contracting States would agree to ask the opinion of an impartial third party, although the final decision would still rest with the States.

43.   The provisions embodied in this Convention, as well as the Commentary related thereto, are the result of close international joint work within the Committee on Fiscal Affairs. A convenient possibility would be to call upon the Committee on Fiscal Affairs to give an opinion on the correct understanding of the provisions where special difficulties of interpretation arise as to particular points. Such a practice, which would be in line with the mandate and aims of the Committee on Fiscal Affairs, might well make a valuable contribution to arriving at a desirable uniformity in the application of the provisions.

44.   It might also be feasible to ask the opinion of certain persons acting as independent arbitrators. In the case of OECD Member countries, the Committee on Fiscal Affairs could, for example, periodically draw up a list of persons from among whom the competent authorities of the two Contracting States concerned could choose the third party to be asked to give an advisory opinion.

RESERVATIONS ON THE ARTICLE

45.   *Portugal* reserves its position on the last sentence of paragraph 1 as it could not accept such a long time limit.

46.   *Portugal, Spain, Turkey* and the *United Kingdom* reserve their positions on the second sentence of paragraph 2. These countries consider that the implementation of reliefs and refunds following a mutual agreement ought to remain linked to time limits prescribed by their domestic laws.

COMMENTARY ON ARTICLE 12
CONCERNING EXCHANGE OF INFORMATION

I. PRELIMINARY REMARKS

1.   There are good grounds for including in a convention for the avoidance of double taxation provisions concerning co-operation between the tax administrations of the two Contracting States. In the first place, it appears to be desirable to give administrative assistance for the purpose of ascertaining facts in relation to which the rules of the convention are to be applied. Moreover, in view of the increasing internationalisation of economic relations, the Contracting States have a growing interest in the reciprocal supply of information on the basis of which domestic taxation laws have to be administered, even if there is no question of the application of any particular Article of the convention.

2.   Therefore, the present Article embodies the rules under which information may be exchanged to the widest possible extent, with a view to laying the proper basis for the implementation of the domestic laws of the Contracting States concerning taxes covered by the Convention and for the application of specific provisions of the Convention. The text of the Article makes it clear that the exchange of information is not restricted by Article 1, so that the information may include particulars about non-domiciled persons.

3.   The matter of administrative assistance for the purpose of tax collection is not dealt with in the Article. This matter often forms the subject of a separate agreement, whether bilateral or multilateral, between the Contracting States. In this context attention is drawn to the Model Convention for mutual administrative assistance in the recovery of tax claims. Alternatively, the provisions on assistance in the field of tax collection may be introduced in a double taxation convention on estates and inheritances and on gifts, whenever Contracting States find it preferable.

4.   Experience in recent years has shown that the text of the Article in the 1966 Estate Tax Draft left room for differing interpretations. Therefore, it was felt desirable to clarify its meaning by a change in the wording of the Article and its Commentary without altering its effects. Apart from a single point of substance (see paragraph 11 below) the main purpose of the changes made has been to remove grounds for divergent interpretations.

II. COMMENTARY ON THE PROVISIONS OF THE ARTICLE

Paragraph 1

5.   The main rule concerning the exchange of information is contained in the first sentence of the paragraph. The competent authorities of the Contracting States shall exchange such information as is necessary to secure the correct application of the provisions of the Convention or of the domestic laws of the Contracting States concerning taxes covered by the Convention even if, in the latter case, a particular Article need not be applied. In order to keep the exchange of information within the framework of the Convention, a limitation is set to the exchange of information so that information should be given only insofar as the national tax in question is covered by the Convention and the taxation under the domestic taxation laws concerned is not contrary to the Convention.

6.   For a typical illustration, reference may be made to the information necessary for the application of Articles 9A and 9B as the methods for eliminating double taxation.

7.   The rule laid down in paragraph 1 allows information to be exchanged in three different ways:

   a) on request, with a special case in mind, it being understood that the regular sources of information available under the domestic taxation procedure should be relied upon in the first instance before a request for information is made to the other State;
   b) automatically, for example, when information about items of capital situated in one Contracting State is transmitted systematically to the other State;
   c) spontaneously, for example, in the case of a State having acquired, through certain investigations, information which it believes to be of interest to the other State.

8.   The manner in which the exchange of information agreed to in the Convention will finally be effected can be decided upon by the competent authorities of the Contracting States.

9.   Reciprocal assistance between tax administrations is feasible only if each administration is assured that the other administration will treat with proper confidence the information which it will receive in the course of their co-operation. At the same time maintenance of such secrecy in the receiving State is a matter of domestic law. It is therefore provided in paragraph 1 that information communicated under the Convention shall be treated as secret in the receiving State in the same manner as information obtained under the domestic law of that State. Sanctions for the violation of such secrecy in that State will be governed by the administrative and penal law of that State.

10.   The information obtained may be disclosed only to persons and authorities involved in the assessment or collection of, the enforcement or prosecution in respect of, or the determination of appeals in relation to, the taxes covered by the Convention. This means that the information may also be communicated to the taxpayer, his proxy or to witnesses. The information received by a Contracting State may be used by such persons or authorities only for the purposes mentioned in paragraph 1. If the information

appears to be of value to the receiving State for purposes other than those referred to, that State may not use the information for such other purposes but it must resort to means specially designed for those purposes (for example, in the case of a non-fiscal crime, to a treaty concerning judicial assistance).

11.   As stated above, the information obtained can be communicated to the persons and authorities mentioned but it does not follow from this that it can be disclosed by them in court sessions held in public or in decisions which reveal the name of the taxpayer. The last sentence of the paragraph, however, opens up this possibility. Once information is used in public court proceedings or in court decisions and thus rendered public, it is clear that from that moment such information can be quoted from the court files or decisions for other purposes even as possible evidence. However, this does not mean that the persons and authorities mentioned in paragraph 1 are allowed to provide on request additional information received. If either or both of the Contracting States object to the information being made public by courts in this way, or, once the information has been made public in this way, to the information being used for other purposes, because this is not the normal procedure under their domestic laws, they should state this expressly in their convention.

Paragraph 2

12.   This paragraph contains certain limitations to the main rule in favour of the requested State. In the first place, the paragraph contains the clarification that a State is not bound to go beyond its own domestic law and administrative practice in putting information at the disposal of the other State. However, types of administrative measures authorised for the purposes of the requested State's tax must be utilised, even though invoked solely to provide information to the other Contracting State. Likewise, domestic provisions concerning tax secrecy should not be interpreted as constituting an obstacle to the exchange of information under the present Article. As mentioned above, the authorities of the requesting State are obliged to observe secrecy with regard to information received under this Article.

13.   Furthermore, the requested State does not need to go so far as to carry out administrative measures that are not permitted under the law or practice of the requesting State or to supply items of information that are not obtainable under the laws or in the normal course of administration of the requesting State. It follows that a State cannot take advantage of the information system of the other State if it is wider than its own system.

14.   Information is deemed to be obtainable in the normal course of administration if it is in the possession of the tax authorities or can be obtained by them in the normal procedure of tax determination, which may include special investigations or special examination of the business accounts kept by the taxpayer or other persons, provided that the tax authorities would make similar investigations or examination for their own purposes. This means that the requested State has to collect the information the other State needs in the same way as if its own taxation was involved, subject to the proviso mentioned in paragraph 13 above.

15.   The requested State is at liberty to refuse to give information in the cases referred to in paragraphs 12 to 14 above. However, if it does give the requested information, it remains within the framework of the agreement on the exchange of information which is laid down in the Convention; consequently it cannot be objected that this State has failed to observe the obligation to secrecy.

16.   If the structure of the information systems of two Contracting States is very different, the conditions under subparagraphs a) and b) of paragraph 2 will lead to the result that the States exchange very little information or perhaps none at all. In such a case, the States may find it appropriate to agree not to invoke paragraph 2 in certain cases or to modify the provisions of paragraph 2 in their bilateral conventions.

17.   In addition to the limitations referred to above, subparagraph *c)* of paragraph 2 contains a reservation concerning the disclosure of certain secret information. Secrets mentioned in this subparagraph should not be taken in too wide a sense. Before invoking this provision, a State should carefully weigh whether the interests of the taxpayer really justify its application. Otherwise, it is clear that too wide an interpretation would in many cases render ineffective the exchange of information provided for in the Convention. The observations made in paragraph 15 above apply here as well. The requested State, in protecting the interests of its taxpayers, is given a certain discretion to refuse the requested information, but if it does supply the information the taxpayer may not claim that the requested State has violated the Convention. It is open to the States to add further dispensations from the obligation to supply information to the items listed in subparagraph *c)*, for example, information protected by provisions on bankers' discretion. It has been felt necessary also to prescribe a limitation with regard to information which concerns the vital interests of the State itself. To this end, it is stipulated that States do not have to supply information the disclosure of which would be contrary to public policy (ordre public).

RESERVATIONS ON THE ARTICLE

18.   *Portugal* reserves the right to apply this Article as drafted in the 1966 Draft Convention (Article 13).

19.   Under the *Swiss* concept, a double taxation convention aims at avoiding international double taxation; the information necessary for the correct application and for the prevention of an abuse of such a convention can be exchanged already within the existing framework of its provisions on the mutual agreement procedure, etc. Switzerland considers a particular provision on the exchange of information as unnecessary since even such an express clause could not, according to the purpose of the convention, provide for more than for an exchange of information necessary for the correct application and prevention of an abuse of the convention. Accordingly, Switzerland has an express reservation on the Article on the exchange of information.

COMMENTARY ON ARTICLE 13
CONCERNING DIPLOMATIC AGENTS AND CONSULAR OFFICERS

1.   The aim of the Article is to secure that diplomatic agents or consular officers shall, under the provisions of a double taxation convention, receive no less favourable treatment than that to which they are entitled under international law or under special international agreements.

2.   The simultaneous application of the provisions of a double taxation convention and of diplomatic and consular privileges confered by virtue of the general rules of international law or under a special international agreement may, under certain circumstances, have the result of discharging, in both Contracting States, tax that would otherwise have been due. In order to avoid tax reliefs that are not intended, Contracting States are free to adopt in their bilateral negotiations an additional provision which may be drafted on the following lines:

"Insofar as, due to fiscal privileges granted to diplomatic agents or consular officers under the general rules of international law or under the provisions of special international agreements, property is not subject to tax in the receiving State, the right to tax shall be reserved to the sending State".

3.   In many Member countries, the domestic law contains provisions to the effect that, while abroad, diplomatic agents and consular officers are treated, for tax purposes, as retaining their domicile in the sending State. In their bilateral negotiations States, in which provisions of this kind are operative, may take a further step by including specific rules that, for the purposes of the convention, establish the sending State as the State of domicile of the members of the diplomatic missions and consular posts of the Contracting States. The special provision suggested here could be drafted as follows:

"Notwithstanding the provisions of Article 4, an individual who is a member of a diplomatic mission, consular post or permanent mission of a Contracting State which is situated in the other Contracting State or in a third State shall be deemed for the purposes of the Convention to be domiciled in the sending State if:

a)   in accordance with international law his estate or gift is not liable to tax in the receiving State in respect of property situated outside that State, and

b)   his total estate or gift is liable to tax in the sending State in the same way as are estates or gifts of persons domiciled in that State."

4.   By virtue of paragraph 1 of Article 4 the diplomatic agents and consular officers of a third State accredited to a Contracting State are not deemed to be domiciled in the receiving State if they are only subject to a limited taxation in that State (see paragraph 16 of the Commentary on Article 4). This consideration also holds true of international organisations established in a Contracting State and their officials if they usually benefit from certain fiscal privileges either under the convention or treaty establishing the organisation or under a treaty between the organisation and the State in which it is established. Contracting States wishing to settle this question expressly, or to prevent undesirable tax reliefs, may add the following provision to this Article:

"The Convention shall not apply to:

a)   gifts made by international organisations or by organs or officials thereof or by persons who are members of a diplomatic mission, consular post or permanent mission of a third State, nor

b)   the estates of such officials or persons, where such organisations, organs, officials or persons are present in a Contracting State and are not treated in either Contracting State as being domiciled there in respect of taxes on estates or gifts."

This means that international organisations, organs or officials who are liable in a Contracting State in respect only of items of property situated therein will not be covered by the Convention.

5   Although honorary consular officers cannot derive from the provisions of the Article any privileges to which they are not entitled under the general rules of international law (there commonly exists only tax exemption for payments received as consideration for expenses honorary consuls have on behalf of the sending State), the Contracting States are free to exclude expressly, by bilateral agreement, honorary consular officers from the application of the Article.

COMMENTARY ON ARTICLE 14
CONCERNING TERRITORIAL EXTENSION

1.   Certain double taxation conventions name the territories to which they apply. Some of them also provide that their provisions may be extended to other territories and define when and how this may be done. A clause of this kind is of particular value to States which have territories overseas or are responsible for the international relations of other States or territories, especially as it recognises that the extension may be effected by an exchange of diplomatic notes. It is also of value when the provisions of the Convention are to be extended to a part of the territory of a Contracting State which was, by special provision, excluded from the application of the Convention. The Article, which provides that the extension may also be effected in any other manner in accordance with the constitutional procedure of the States, is drafted in a form acceptable from the constitutional point of view of all Member countries affected by the provision in question. The only prior condition for the extension of a convention to any States or territories is that they must impose taxes substantially similar in character to those to which the Convention applies.

2.   The Article provides that the Convention may be extended either in its entirety or with any necessary modifications, that the extension takes effect from such date and subject to such conditions as may be agreed between the Contracting States and, finally, that the termination of the Convention automatically terminates its application to any States or territories to which it has been extended, unless otherwise agreed by the Contracting States.

COMMENTARY ON ARTICLES 15 AND 16
CONCERNING ENTRY INTO FORCE AND TERMINATION

1.   The present provisions on the procedure for entry into force, ratification and termination are drafted for bilateral conventions and correspond to the rules usually contained in international treaties.

2.   Some Contracting States may need an additional provision in the first paragraph of Article 15 indicating the authorities which have to give their consent to the ratification. Other States may agree that the Article should indicate that the entry into force takes place after an exchange of notes confirming that each State has completed the procedures required for such entry into force.

3.   It is open to Contracting States to agree that the convention shall enter into force when a specified period has elapsed after the exchange of the instruments of ratification or after the confirmation that each State has completed the procedures required for such entry into force.

4.   No provisions have been drafted as to the date on which the convention shall have effect or cease to have effect, since such provisions would largely depend on the domestic laws of the Contracting States concerned. It seems that the best solution is to express the date on which the effect of the convention shall begin or cease by reference to the date of the taxable event (death or gift).

5.   As it is of advantage that the convention should remain in force at least for a certain period, the Article on termination provides that notice of termination can only be given after a certain year, to be fixed by bilateral agreement. It is open to the Contracting States to decide upon the earliest year during which such notice can be given or even to agree not to fix any such year, if they so desire.

RECOMMENDATION OF THE COUNCIL
CONCERNING THE AVOIDANCE OF DOUBLE TAXATION
WITH RESPECT TO TAXES ON ESTATES AND INHERITANCES AND ON GIFTS

(Adopted by the Council at the 563rd Meeting on 3rd June, 1982)

The Council,

Having regard to Article 5(b) of the Convention on the Organisation for Economic Co-operation and Development of 14th December, 1960;

Having regard to the Recommendations of the Council of 28th June, 1966 concerning the Avoidance of Double Taxation with respect to taxes on Estates and Inheritances and of 11th April, 1977 concerning the Avoidance of Double Taxation with respect to Taxes on Income and on Capital;

Having regard to the Report of the Committee on Fiscal Affairs of 3rd March, 1982 on the OECD Convention for the Avoidance of Double Taxation with respect to Taxes on Estates and Inheritances and on Gifts.

Considering the desirability of extending to taxes on estates and inheritances and on gifts the efforts of Member countries with regard to the elimination of double taxation and of concluding Conventions between them for that purpose;

Considering also the need to harmonize existing bilateral conventions on the basis of uniform principles, definitions, rules and methods, to agree on a common interpretation and to extend the existing network of such conventions to all Member countries;

Considering that the new Model Convention will make it possible to confirm and extend the existing international co-operation in tax matters;

I.   RECOMMENDS to the Governments of Member countries:

   1.   to pursue their efforts to conclude bilateral conventions for the avoidance of double taxation with respect to taxes on estates and inheritances or on gifts with those Member countries with which they have not yet entered into such conventions and to revise those of existing conventions between them which may no longer be in keeping with present-day needs;
   2.   when concluding new bilateral conventions or revising existing bilateral conventions between them, to conform to the Model Convention set out in the Annex hereto as interpreted by the Commentaries thereto and having regard to the reservations to the Model Convention, which are contained in the Report referred to above.

II.   REQUESTS the Governments of Member countries to notify the Organisation of the text of any new or revised double taxation convention concluded with each other and, where appropriate, the reasons why the provisions of the Model Convention have not been adopted in such conventions.

III.   INSTRUCTS the Committee on Fiscal Affairs:

1. to examine the notifications so supplied and to report to it as appropriate;
2. conduct periodic reviews of situations where double taxation may occur, in the light of experience gained by Member countries, and to make appropriate proposals for its removal.

IV.   DECIDES to repeal the Recommendation of the Council of 28th June, 1966 referred to above.

Appendix II

LIST OF DOUBLE TAXATION CONVENTIONS ON ESTATES AND INHERITANCES AND GIFTS SIGNED BETWEEN OECD MEMBER COUNTRIES

(as of 1-7-1981)

Contracting States	Date of preceding convention	Date of signature	Date of protocols supplementary convention etc.	Gifts taxes	Taxes on estates and inheritances
1. Germany-Greece	New	18.11.10 / 1.12.10	Exch. of notes: 12/3/53-6/5/53 14/6/54-28/9/54		X
2. Greece-Spain	New	6.03.19	Exch. of notes: 15/1/53-3/2/53		X
3. Germany-Sweden	New	14.05.35			X
4. France-Sweden	New	24.12.36	Sup. 8.4.49 Conv. 1.1.63		X
5. Norway-United States	New	13.06.49			X
6. Ireland-United States	New	13.09.49			X
7. Norway-Sweden	New	17.12.49			X
8. Greece-United States	New	20.02.50	Sup. 18.7.53 Prot. 12.2.64		X
9. Finland-Sweden	New	31.03.50			X
10. Canada-France	New	16.03.51			X
11. Switzerland-United States	New	9.07.51			X
12. Netherlands-Switzerland	New	12.11.51			X
13. Finland-United States	New	3.03.52			X
14. Netherlands-Sweden	New	25.04.52			X
15. Denmark-Sweden	New	27.10.53			X
16. France Switzerland	New	31.12.53	Sup.c.29.08.73		X
17. Finland-Netherlands	New	29.3.54			X
18. Finland-Norway	New	29.03.54			X
19. Japan-United States	New	16.04.54		X	X
20. Belgium-United States	New	27.05.54 (not in force)			X
21. Austria-Germany	28.05.22	04.10.54			X
22. Canada-Ireland	New	28.10.54			X
23. Italy-United States	New	30.03.55			X
24. Belgium-Sweden	New	18.01.56			X
25. Denmark-Norway	New	23.05.56			X

	Signature	Entry into force		
30. Finland-France	New	25.08.58		X
31. Belgium-France	New	20.01.59		X
32. Austria-France*	4.05.51 30.05.51	8.10.59		X
33. Canada-United States	8.06.44	17.02.61		X
34. Austria-Sweden	New	21.11.62		X
35. France-Spain*	New	8.01.63		X
36. Spain-Sweden	New	25.04.63		X
37. France-United Kingdom	New	21.06.63		X
38. Italy-Greece	New	13.02.64		X
39. Italy-United Kingdom	New	15.02.66		X
40. Denmark-Italy	New	10.03.66		X
41. Netherlands-United States	New	15.07.69		X
42. Denmark-Switzerland	14.01.57	23.11.73		X
43. Austria-Switzerland*	17.08.46	30.01.74		X
44. Denmark-Finland	12.11.53 18.07.55	30.09.75		X
45. Ireland-United Kingdom	29.03.23+Pr.	07.12.77	X	
46. United States-United Kingdom	14.04.23 16.04.45	19.10.78	X	X
47. Germany-Switzerland	15.07.31	30.11.78	X	X
48. France-United States	18.10.46+Pr. 17/5/48-22/6/56	24.11.78		X
49. Sweden-Switzerland	16.10.48	7.02.79 (not in force)		X
50. Netherlands-United Kingdom	15.10.48	11.12.79	X	X
51. Sweden-United Kingdom	14.10.64	8.10.80	X	X
52. Germany-United States	New	3.12.80 (not in force)		X

* Conventions on income and capital and on estates and inheritances.

137

THE 1966 DRAFT CONVENTION

Chapter I

SCOPE OF THE CONVENTION

Article 1
ESTATES COVERED

This Convention shall apply to estates of deceased persons whose domicile at their death was in one or both of the Contracting States.

Article 2
TAXES COVERED

1.   This Convention shall apply to taxes on estates and inheritances imposed on behalf of each Contracting States or of its political sub-divisions or local authorities, irrespective of the manner in which they are levied.

2.   There shall be regarded as taxes on estates and inheritances all taxes imposed on the occasion of death in the form of tax on the corpus of the estate, of tax on inheritances, of transfer duties, or of taxes on donations *mortis causa.*

3.   The existing taxes to which the Convention shall apply are, in particular:

   a)   in the case of (State A): ......
   b)   in the case of (State B): ......

4.   The Convention shall also apply to any taxes on estates and inheritances which are subsequently imposed in addition to, or in place of, the existing taxes. At the end of each year, the competent authorities of the Contracting States shall notify to each other any changes which have been made in their respective taxation laws.

Chapter II

DEFINITIONS

Article 3

GENERAL DEFINITIONS

1.   In this Convention:

   a)   the terms "a Contracting State" and "the other Contracting State" mean (State A) or (State B), as the context requires;
   b)   the term "competent authority" means:
      1.   in (State A) ......
      2.   in (State B) ......

2.   As regards the application of the Convention by a Contracting State, any term not otherwise defined shall, unless the context otherwise requires, have the meaning which it has under the laws of that Contracting State relating to the taxes which are the subject of the Convention.

Article 4

FISCAL DOMICILE

1.   For the purposes of this Convention, the question whether a person at his death was domiciled in a Contracting State shall be determined according to the law of that State.

2.   Where by reason of the provisions of paragraph 1 a person was domiciled in both Contracting States, then this case shall be determined in accordance with the following rules:

   a)   He shall be deemed to have been domiciled in the Contracting State in which he had a permanent home available to him. If he had a permanent home available to him in both Contracting States, the domicile shall be deemed to be in the Contracting State with which his personal and economic relations were closest (centre of vital interests);
   b)   If the Contracting State in which he had his centre of vital interests cannot be determined, or if he had not a permanent home available to him in either Contracting State, the domicile shall be deemed to be in the Contracting State in which he had an habitual abode;
   c)   If he had an habitual abode in both Contracting States or in neither of them, the domicile shall be deemed to be in the Contracting State of which he was a national;
   c)   If he was a national of both Contracting State or of neither of them, the competent authorities of the Contracting States shall settle the question by mutual agreement.

Chapter III

TAXING RULES

Article 5

IMMOVABLE PROPERTY

1.   Immovable property may be taxed in the Contracting State in which such property is situated.

2.   The term "immovable property" shall be defined in accordance with the law of the Contracting State in which the property in question is situated. The term shall in any case include property accessory to immovable property, livestock and equipment used in agriculture and forestry, rights to which the provisions of general law respecting landed property apply, usufruct of immovable property and rights to variable or fixed payments as consideration for the working of, or the right to work, mineral deposits, sources and other natural resources; ships, boats and aircraft shall not be regarded as immovable property.

3.   The provisions of paragraphs 1 and 2 shall also apply to immovable property of an enterprise and to immovable property used for the performance of professional services or other independent activities of a similar character.

Article 6

BUSINESS PROPERTY OF A PERMANENT ESTABLISHMENT
AND ASSETS PERTAINING TO A FIXED BASE USED
FOR THE PERFORMANCE OF PROFESSIONAL SERVICES

1.   Except for assets referred to in Articles 5 and 7, assets forming part of the business property of a permanent establishment of an enterprise may be taxed in the Contracting State in which the permanent establishment is situated.

2.   The term "permanent establishment" means a fixed place of business in which the business of the enterprise is wholly or partly carried on.

3.   The term "permanent establishment" shall include especially:
   a)   a place of management;
   b)   a branch;
   c)   an office;
   d)   a factory;
   e)   a workshop;
   f)   a mine, quarry or other place of extraction of natural resources;
   g)   a building site or construction or assembly project which exists for more than twelve months.

4.   The term "permanent establishment" shall not be deemed to include:

   a) the use of facilities solely for the purpose of storage, display or delivery of goods or merchandise belonging to the enterprise;
   b) the maintenance of a stock of goods or merchandise belonging to the enterprise solely for the purpose of storage, display or delivery;
   c) the maintenance of a stock of goods or merchandise belonging to the enterprise solely for the purpose of processing by another enterprise;
   d) the maintenance of a fixed place of business solely for the purpose of purchasing goods or merchandise, or for collecting information, for the enterprise;
   e) the maintenance of a fixed place of business solely for the purpose of advertising, for the supply of information, for scientific research or for similar activities which have a preparatory or auxiliary character, for the enterprise.

5.   A person acting in a Contracting State on behalf of an enterprise of the other Contracting State – other than an agent of an independent status to whom paragraph 6 applies – shall be deemed to be a permanent establishment in the first-mentioned State if he has, and habitually exercises in that State, an authority to conclude contracts in the name of the enterprise, unless his activities are limited to the purchase of goods or merchandise for the enterprise.

6.   An enterprise of a Contracting State shall not be deemed to have a permanent establishment in the other Contracting State merely because it carries on business in that other State through a broker, general commission agent or any other agent of an independent status, where such persons are acting in the ordinary course of their business.

7.   Except for assets described in Article 5, assets pertaining to a fixed base used for the performance of professional services or other independent activities of a similar character may be taxed in the Contracting State in which the fixed base is situated.

Article 7

SHIPS, BOATS AND AIRCRAFT

1.   Ships and aircraft operated in international traffic and boats engaged in inland waterways transport, and movable property pertaining to the operation of such ships, aircraft and boats, may be taxed in the Contracting State in which the place of effective management of the enterprise is situated.

Article 8

PROPERTY NOT EXPRESSLY MENTIONED

1.   Property other than property referred to in Articles 5,6 and 7 shall be taxable only in the Contracting State in which the deceased was domiciled at his death.

Article 9

DEDUCTION OF DEBTS

1.   Debts especially secured on any property referred to in Article 5 shall be deducted from the value of that property. Debts, not being especially secured on any property referred to in Article 5, which are represented by the acquisition, conversion, repair or upkeep of any such property, shall be deducted from the value of that property.

2.   Subject to paragraph 1, debts pertaining to a permanent establishment of an enterprise or to a fixed base used for the performance of professional services or other independent activities of a similar character, and debts pertaining to any business of shipping, inland-waterways transport or air transport, shall be deducted from the value of property referred to in Article 6 or Article 7, as the case may be.

3.   Other debts shall be deducted from the value of property to which Article 8 applies.

4.   If a debt exceeds the value of the property from which it is deductible in a Contracting State, according to paragraphs 1, 2 and 3, the excess shall be deducted from the value of any other property taxable in that State.

5.   Any excess still remaining after the deductions referred to in the preceding paragraphs shall be deducted from the value of the property liable to tax in the other Contracting State.

Chapter IV

METHODS FOR ELIMINATION OF DOUBLE TAXATION

Article 10A
EXEMPTION METHOD

1.   The Contracting State in which the deceased was domiciled at his death shall exempt from tax property which, in accordance with the provisions of this Convention, may be taxed in the other Contracting State but may, in calculating tax on any property which it remains entitled to tax, apply the rate of tax which would have been applicable if the exempted property had not been so exempted.

Article 10B
CREDIT METHOD

1.   The Contracting State in which the deceased was domiciled at his death shall deduct from the tax calculated according to its law an amount equal to the tax paid in the other Contracting State on property which, in accordance with the provisions of this Convention, may be taxed in the other State.

2.   The deduction shall not, however, exceed that part of the tax, as computed before the deduction is given, which is appropriate to the property which may be taxed in the other Contracting State.

Chapter V

SPECIAL PROVISIONS

Article 11

NON-DISCRIMINATION

1.   The nationals of a Contracting State shall not be subjected in the other Contracting State to any taxation or any requirement connected therewith which is other or more burdensome than the taxation and connected requirements to which nationals of that other State in the same circumstances are or may be subjected.

2.   The term "nationals" means:
    a)   all individuals possessing the nationality of a Contracting State;
    b)   all legal persons, partnerships and associations deriving their status as such from the law in force in a Contracting State.

3.   Stateless persons shall not be subjected in a Contracting State to any taxation or any requirement connected therewith which is other or more burdensome than the taxation and connected requirements to which nationals of that State in the same circumstances are or may be subjected.

4.   The taxation on a permanent establishment which an enterprise of a Contracting State has in the other Contracting State shall not be less favourably levied in that other State than the taxation levied on enterprises of that other State carrying on the same activities.
    This provision shall not be construed as obliging a Contracting State to grant to residents of the other Contracting State any personal allowances, reliefs and reductions for taxation purposes on account of civil status or family responsibilities which it grants to its own residents.

5.   Enterprises of a Contracting State, the capital of which is wholly or partly owned or controlled, directly or indirectly, by one or more residents of the other Contracting State, shall not be subjected in the first-mentioned Contracting State to any taxation or any requirement connected therewith which is other or more burdensome than the taxation and connected requirements to which other similar enterprises of that first-mentioned State are or may be subjected.

6.   In this Article the term "taxation" means taxes of every kind and description.

Article 12

MUTUAL AGREEMENT PROCEDURE

1.   Any person who considers that the actions of one or both of the Contracting States result or will result for him in taxation not in accordance with this Convention may, notwithstanding the remedies provided by the national laws of those States, present his case to the competent authority of either State.

2.   The competent authority shall endeavour, if the objection appears to it to be justified and if it is not itself able to arrive at an appropriate solution, to resolve the case by mutual agreement with the competent authority of the other Contracting State, with a view to the avoidance of taxation not in accordance with the Convention.

3.   The competent authorities of the Contracting States shall endeavour to resolve by mutual agrement any difficulties or doubts arising as to the interpretation or application of the Convention. They may also consult together for the elimination of double taxation in cases not provided for in the Convention.

4.   The competent authorities of the Contracting States may communicate with each other directly for the purpose of reaching an agreement in the sense of the preceding paragraphs. When it seems advisable in order to reach agreement to have an oral exchange of opinions, such exchange may take place through a Commission consisting of representatives of the competent authorities of the Contracting States.

Article 13

EXCHANGE OF INFORMATION

1.   The competent authorities of the Contracting States shall exchange such information as is necessary for the carrying out of this Convention and of the domestic laws of the Contracting States concerning taxes covered by this Convention insofar as the taxation therunder is in accordance with this Convention. Any information so exchanged shall be treated as secret and shall not be disclosed to any persons or authorities other than those concerned with the assessment or collection of the taxes which are the subject of the Convention.

2.   In no case shall the provisions of paragraph 1 be construed so as to impose on one of the Contracting States the obligation:

   a)   to carry out administrative measures at variance with the laws or the administrative practice of that or of the other Contracting State;

   b)   to supply particulars which are not obtainable under the laws or in the normal course of the administration of that or of the other Contracting State;

   c)   to supply information which would disclose any trade, business, industrial, commercial or professional secret or trade process, or information the disclosure of which would be contrary to public policy (ordre public).

Article 14

DIPLOMATIC AND CONSULAR OFFICIALS

Nothing in this Convention shall affect the fiscal privileges of diplomatic or consular officials under the general rules of international law or under the provisions of special agreements.

Article 15

TERRITORIAL EXTENSION

1.   This Convention may be extended, either in its entirety or with any necessary modifications, [to any part of the territory of (State A) or of (State B) which is specifically excluded from the application of the Convention or] to any State or territory for whose international relations (State A) or (State B) is responsible, which imposes taxes substantially similar in character to those to which the Convention applies. Any such extension shall take effect

from such date and subject to such modifications and conditions, including conditions as to termination, as may be specified and agreed between the Contracting States in notes to be exchanged through diplomatic channels or in any other manner in accordance with their constitutional procedures.

2.   Unless otherwise agreed by both Contracting States, the denunciation of the Convention by one of them under Article 17 shall terminate, in the manner provided for in that Article, the application of the Convention [to any part of the territory of (State A) or of (State B) or] to any State or territory to which it has been extended under this Article.

Note: The words between brackets are of relevance when, by special provision, a part of the territory of a Contracting State is excluded from the application of the Convention.

Chapter VI

FINAL PROVISIONS

Article 16

ENTRY INTO FORCE

1.   This Convention shall be ratified and the instruments of ratification shall be exchanged at ...... as soon as possible.

2.   The Convention shall enter into force on the day on which the instruments of ratification are exchanged and its provision shall have effect in relation to estates of persons dying on or after that day.

Article 17

TERMINATION

This Convention shall remain in force until denounced by one of the Contracting States. Either Contracting State may denounce the Convention, through diplomatic channels, with effect from the end of any calendar year not earlier than the year ...... by giving at least six months notice of termination. In such an event, the Convention will not apply to estates of persons who died after the expiry of the calendar year with respect to the end of which the Convention has been denounced.

TERMINAL CLAUSE

Note: The terminal clause concerning the signing shall be drafted in accordance with the constitutional procedure of both Contracting States.

OECD SALES AGENTS
DÉPOSITAIRES DES PUBLICATIONS DE L'OCDE

ARGENTINA – ARGENTINE
Carlos Hirsch S.R.L., Florida 165, 4° Piso (Galería Guemes)
1333 BUENOS AIRES, Tel. 33.1787.2391 y 30.7122
AUSTRALIA – AUSTRALIE
Australia and New Zealand Book Company Pty, Ltd.,
10 Aquatic Drive, Frenchs Forest, N.S.W. 2086
P.O. Box 459, BROOKVALE, N.S.W. 2100
AUSTRIA – AUTRICHE
OECD Publications and Information Center
4 Simrockstrasse 5300 BONN. Tel. (0228) 21.60.45
Local Agent/Agent local :
Gerold and Co., Graben 31, WIEN 1. Tel. 52.22.35
BELGIUM – BELGIQUE
CCLS – LCLS
19, rue Plantin, 1070 BRUXELLES. Tel. 02.521.04.73
BRAZIL – BRÉSIL
Mestre Jou S.A., Rua Guaipa 518,
Caixa Postal 24090, 05089 SAO PAULO 10. Tel. 261.1920
Rua Senador Dantas 19 s/205-6, RIO DE JANEIRO GB.
Tel. 232.07.32
CANADA
Renouf Publishing Company Limited,
2182 St. Catherine Street West,
MONTRÉAL, Que. H3H 1M7. Tel. (514)937.3519
OTTAWA, Ont. K1P 5A6, 61 Sparks Street
DENMARK – DANEMARK
Munksgaard Export and Subscription Service
35, Nørre Søgade
DK 1370 KØBENHAVN K. Tel. +45.1.12.85.70
FINLAND – FINLANDE
Akateeminen Kirjakauppa
Keskuskatu 1, 00100 HELSINKI 10. Tel. 65.11.22
FRANCE
Bureau des Publications de l'OCDE,
2 rue André-Pascal, 75775 PARIS CEDEX 16. Tel. (1) 524.81.67
Principal correspondant :
13602 AIX-EN-PROVENCE : Librairie de l'Université.
Tel. 26.18.08
GERMANY – ALLEMAGNE
OECD Publications and Information Center
4 Simrockstrasse 5300 BONN Tel. (0228) 21.60.45
GREECE – GRÈCE
Librairie Kauffmann, 28 rue du Stade,
ATHÈNES 132. Tel. 322.21.60
HONG-KONG
Government Information Services,
Publications/Sales Section, Baskerville House,
2/F., 22 Ice House Street
ICELAND – ISLANDE
Snaebjörn Jönsson and Co., h.f.,
Hafnarstraeti 4 and 9, P.O.B. 1131, REYKJAVIK.
Tel. 13133/14281/11936
INDIA – INDE
Oxford Book and Stationery Co. :
NEW DELHI-1, Scindia House. Tel. 45896
CALCUTTA 700016, 17 Park Street. Tel. 240832
INDONESIA – INDONÉSIE
PDIN-LIPI, P.O. Box 3065/JKT., JAKARTA, Tel. 583467
IRELAND – IRLANDE
TDC Publishers – Library Suppliers
12 North Frederick Street, DUBLIN 1 Tel. 744835-749677
ITALY – ITALIE
Libreria Commissionaria Sansoni :
Via Lamarmora 45, 50121 FIRENZE. Tel. 579751/584468
Via Bartolini 29, 20155 MILANO. Tel. 365083
Sub-depositari :
Ugo Tassi
Via A. Farnese 28, 00192 ROMA. Tel. 310590
Editrice e Libreria Herder,
Piazza Montecitorio 120, 00186 ROMA. Tel. 6794628
Costantino Ercolano, Via Generale Orsini 46, 80132 NAPOLI. Tel.
405210
Libreria Hoepli, Via Hoepli 5, 20121 MILANO. Tel. 865446
Libreria Scientifica, Dott. Lucio de Biasio "Aeiou"
Via Meravigli 16, 20123 MILANO Tel. 807679
Libreria Zanichelli
Piazza Galvani 1/A, 40124 Bologna Tel. 237389
Libreria Lattes, Via Garibaldi 3, 10122 TORINO. Tel. 519274
La diffusione delle edizioni OCSE è inoltre assicurata dalle migliori
librerie nelle città più importanti.
JAPAN – JAPON
OECD Publications and Information Center,
Landic Akasaka Bldg., 2-3-4 Akasaka,
Minato-ku, TOKYO 107 Tel. 586.2016
KOREA – CORÉE
Pan Korea Book Corporation,
P.O. Box n° 101 Kwangwhamun, SÉOUL. Tel. 72.7369

LEBANON – LIBAN
Documenta Scientifica/Redico,
Edison Building, Bliss Street, P.O. Box 5641, BEIRUT.
Tel. 354429 – 344425
MALAYSIA – MALAISIE
and/et SINGAPORE - SINGAPOUR
University of Malaya Co-operative Bookshop Ltd.
P.O. Box 1127, Jalan Pantai Baru
KUALA LUMPUR. Tel. 51425, 54058, 54361
THE NETHERLANDS – PAYS-BAS
Staatsuitgeverij
Verzendboekhandel Chr. Plantijnstraat 1
Postbus 20014
2500 EA S-GRAVENHAGE. Tel. nr. 070.789911
Voor bestellingen: Tel. 070.789208
NEW ZEALAND – NOUVELLE-ZÉLANDE
Publications Section,
Government Printing Office Bookshops:
AUCKLAND: Retail Bookshop: 25 Rutland Street,
Mail Orders: 85 Beach Road, Private Bag C.P.O.
HAMILTON: Retail Ward Street,
Mail Orders, P.O. Box 857
WELLINGTON: Retail: Mulgrave Street (Head Office),
Cubacade World Trade Centre
Mail Orders: Private Bag
CHRISTCHURCH: Retail: 159 Hereford Street,
Mail Orders: Private Bag
DUNEDIN: Retail: Princes Street
Mail Order: P.O. Box 1104
NORWAY – NORVÈGE
J.G. TANUM A/S Karl Johansgate 43
P.O. Box 1177 Sentrum OSLO 1. Tel. (02) 80.12.60
PAKISTAN
Mirza Book Agency, 65 Shahrah Quaid-E-Azam, LAHORE 3.
Tel. 66839
PHILIPPINES
National Book Store, Inc.
Library Services Division, P.O. Box 1934, MANILA.
Tel. Nos. 49.43.06 to 09, 40.53.45, 49.45.12
PORTUGAL
Livraria Portugal, Rua do Carmo 70-74,
1117 LISBOA CODEX. Tel. 360582/3
SPAIN – ESPAGNE
Mundi-Prensa Libros, S.A.
Castelló 37, Apartado 1223, MADRID-1. Tel. 275.46.55
Libreria Bosch, Ronda Universidad 11, BARCELONA 7.
Tel. 317.53.08, 317.53.58
SWEDEN – SUÈDE
AB CE Fritzes Kungl Hovbokhandel,
Box 16 356, S 103 27 STH, Regeringsgatan 12,
DS STOCKHOLM. Tel. 08/23.89.00
SWITZERLAND – SUISSE
OECD Publications and Information Center
4 Simrockstrasse 5300 BONN. Tel. (0228) 21.60.45
Local Agents/Agents locaux
Librairie Payot, 6 rue Grenus, 1211 GENÈVE 11. Tel. 022.31.89.50
TAIWAN – FORMOSE
Good Faith Worldwide Int'l Co., Ltd.
9th floor, No. 118, Sec. 2
Chung Hsiao E. Road
TAIPEI. Tel. 391.7396/391.7397
THAILAND – THAILANDE
Suksit Siam Co., Ltd., 1715 Rama IV Rd,
Samyan, BANGKOK 5. Tel. 2511630
TURKEY – TURQUIE
Kültur Yayinlari Is-Türk Ltd. Sti.
Atatürk Bulvari No : 77/B
KIZILAY/ANKARA. Tel. 17 02 66
Dolmabahce Cad. No : 29
BESIKTAS/ISTANBUL. Tel. 60 71 88
UNITED KINGDOM – ROYAUME-UNI
H.M. Stationery Office, P.O.B. 569,
LONDON SE1 9NH. Tel. 01.928.6977, Ext. 410 or
49 High Holborn, LONDON WC1V 6 HB (personal callers)
Branches at: EDINBURGH, BIRMINGHAM, BRISTOL,
MANCHESTER, BELFAST.
UNITED STATES OF AMERICA – ÉTATS-UNIS
OECD Publications and Information Center, Suite 1207,
1750 Pennsylvania Ave., N.W. WASHINGTON, D.C.20006 – 4582
Tel. (202) 724.1857
VENEZUELA
Libreria del Este, Avda. F. Miranda 52, Edificio Galipan,
CARACAS 106. Tel. 32.23.01/33.26.04/33.24.73
YUGOSLAVIA – YOUGOSLAVIE
Jugoslovenska Knjiga, Terazije 27, P.O.B. 36, BEOGRAD.
Tel. 621.992

Les commandes provenant de pays où l'OCDE n'a pas encore désigné de dépositaire peuvent être adressées à :
OCDE, Bureau des Publications, 2, rue André-Pascal, 75775 PARIS CEDEX 16.
Orders and inquiries from countries where sales agents have not yet been appointed may be sent to:
OECD, Publications Office, 2 rue André-Pascal, 75775 PARIS CEDEX 16.

65958-12-1982

OECD PUBLICATIONS, 2, rue André-Pascal, 75775 PARIS CEDEX 16 - No. 42393 1983
PRINTED IN FRANCE
(23 83 02 1) ISBN 92-64-12403-9